CLICKS
HOW TO BE YOUR
BEST SELF ONLINE

ABOUT THE AUTHOR

Natasha Devon MBE tours schools, colleges and universities throughout the world delivering talks and conducting research on mental health and related issues. She is an ambassador for the charity Glitch (which promotes digital citizenship and seeks to protect marginalised voices online) and a patron for No Panic (an organization helping people manage anxiety). She has founded several campaigns including the Mental Health Media Charter and Where's Your Head At? which aims to improve mental health in work places. She lives in London and loves yoga, books and all cheeses apart from the gross ones with veins.

Other books by Natasha Devon

Yes You Can: Ace School Without Losing Your Mind

A Beginner's Guide to Being Mental: An A-Z

Toxic

CLICKS
HOW TO BE YOUR
BEST SELF ONLINE
NATASHA
DEVON

Featuring illustrations by Rubyetc

MACMILLAN

Published 2023 by Macmillan Children's Books
an imprint of Pan Macmillan
The Smithson, 6 Briset Street, London EC1M 5NR
EU representative: Macmillan Publishers Ireland Ltd, 1st Floor,
The Liffey Trust Centre, 117–126 Sheriff Street Upper
Dublin 1, D01 YC43
Associated companies throughout the world
www.panmacmillan.com

ISBN 978-1-5290-6663-0

1 3 5 7 9 8 6 4 2

A CIP catalogue record for this book is available from the British Library.

Printed and bound by CPI Group (UK) Ltd, Croydon CR0 4YY

CONTENTS

INTRODUCTION

THE INVENTION OF THE INTERNET

should have been a glorious, utopian, giant leap forward in the progress and evolution of humankind. And in many ways, it was. The idea that we are no longer restricted by geographical boundaries, that if we want to know what the world's leading scientists think about climate change, or what the weather is like in Outer Mongolia, or when the next series of our favourite show is coming out we can simply ask a tiny device we keep in our pockets would be astounding to anyone who died before about 1990.

Now, I appreciate if you're reading this, the likelihood is you were born quite a bit after 1990, therefore it probably feels like aeons ago, from your perspective.

So, let me put this into context: humans have been present on Earth for approximately 200,000 years.

The internet was invented in 1960, so has been around approximately 1/3000th of that time.

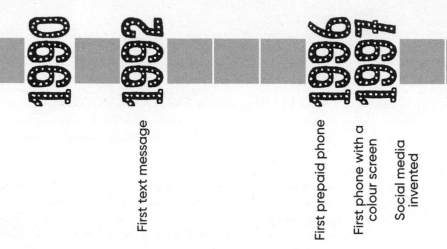

1990

1992 First text message

1996 First prepaid phone

1997 First phone with a colour screen / Social media invented

Social media was invented in 1997, **smartphones** in 2001, but they only really took off after **iPhones** came onto the market in 2007.

That means, actually, the ability to use and access the internet as we do today – constantly and on the fly – has really only been present for about 1/12500th of human history. No wonder we're so bad at it.

Social media should make us more connected, less lonely, kinder and more empathetic towards our fellow humans, plugging us in as it does to (at least theoretically) three billion other users from all over the globe. Yet, anyone who has been paying attention for the past couple of years knows it hasn't quite panned out that way. The internet is awash with false information and it's increasingly difficult to separate it from the truth. Social media platforms have become a tool used by various groups who want to influence the way we behave, what we believe and who we feel inclined to vote for. Meanwhile, users have become increasingly extreme and polarized in their opinions, which has caused (in some cases) unmendable rifts in families and friendship groups.

2001

Smartphones
invented

2007

The first iPhone

But I realize, even as I type these words, that knowing this isn't enough to make the average person delete their social media accounts and lock their smartphone in a drawer.

How do I know this? Because I've spent the past year of my life researching all the ways tech messes with our brains and manipulates our emotions and behaviours, and whilst I've been shocked, appalled and alarmed, none of it has been sufficient to inspire me to delete my social media accounts and lock my phone away in a drawer.

Like most people, I find it hard to imagine life without my phone and I'm just not sure how (or even if) I could survive and thrive if it was ever taken away. It's not just the FOMO that would get me, it would be the absence of apps that make our lives easier, the dearth of instantaneous information, not being able to access music and books wherever I happen to be, or being unable to instantaneously WhatsApp a random thought to a friend (which I know will have fallen out of my head by the end of the day). These are all part of the way I live now.

5

Tech has, for most of us, inched its way into every aspect of our lives. Trying to extract it would be like attempting to remove the eggs from a baked cake, i.e. pretty much impossible. And, let's face it, tech isn't all bad. **For every person who has been trolled, cyberbullied, radicalized or taken in by fake news on the internet, there's another who has found their tribe, made money as a blogger or YouTuber, been inspired by an online role model, started a world-changing campaign or accessed support for their mental health.**

So, this is not a book designed to scare the tits off you about the various dangers of the online world. If what I hear from you during my day job visiting schools all over the globe is anything to judge by, you get enough of that already. **This is a book about how to navigate online life**. It will teach you to be vigilant against some of the potential pitfalls but also how to use the internet to your advantage, to make your voice heard and bring about the types of changes you'd like to see.

In order to do this, it will be necessary to understand what tech actually does to our brains and how it's being harnessed for evil by people with dodgy intentions. But, rest assured, the conclusion of this book will not be:

It will be:

Or something a bit pithier, along those lines . . .

SOCIAL MEDIA AND ME

One of the skills I will be encouraging you to develop in this book is investigating the motivations and backgrounds of people providing you with information, so you can make an assessment about any potential biases they might have. (To have a 'bias' is to think of one person or group in either a favourable or an unfavourable way, which can then make the way you treat them unfair. Most of our biases are 'unconscious', i.e. based on beliefs we've absorbed from the world around us and that we don't really notice.) I think it's only fair, then, that I give you a potted (browsing) history of my relationship with social media and the internet.

I got my first mobile phone when I was eighteen, just before I left sixth form. By today's standards, it was a laughable, plastic brick of a thing, which could only be used for calls and texts. I still remember the first time I ever got a text message. I had absolutely no idea what they were and was like:

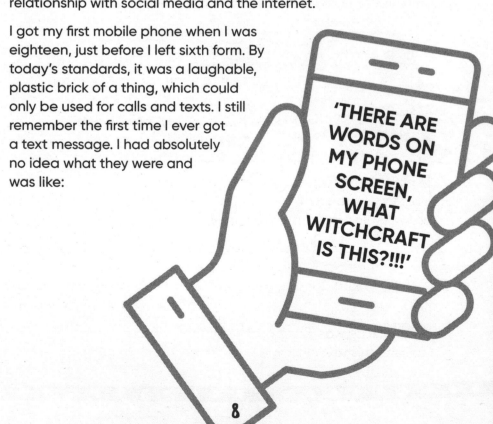

'THERE ARE WORDS ON MY PHONE SCREEN, WHAT WITCHCRAFT IS THIS?!!!'

After discovering the answer to that question,
I developed a pretty hardcore texting addiction.

I LOVED texting.

I couldn't get enough of it.

The idea that you could spontaneously pop
a thought you'd had into someone else's
consciousness, any time, was like catnip to me.
All through uni, I texted like a fiend.

I noticed I'd feel freer to say what was really
on my mind over text, because it eliminated the
awkwardness of having to articulate things orally,
or (God forbid) face-to-face.

I sent ill-advised drunken texts, then
texted apologies the next morning
with a clouting hangover.

I'd sometimes be inspired to send what
were essentially text essays to people outlining
some deep, philosophical ponderings and,

since back then there was a limit on how many
characters you could send in one go, they'd often
arrive in bewildering, out-of-sequence chunks.

I had text flirtations with girlfriends, boyfriends and
randomers I'd met at the student union the night before
whilst dancing to S Club 7 (look them up. And before you
ask, the answer is 'yes, really').

My catchphrase was 'hang on, I've just
got to send this text message!'.

Despite all this texting action, my academic life was much more antiquated. We had a 'computer room' in our halls of residence which I'd pop into about once a week to send an email to my mum reassuring her I was:

- **eating vegetables** ←
- **getting enough sleep** ←
- **absolutely not snogging people whose names I didn't know**

(all lies)

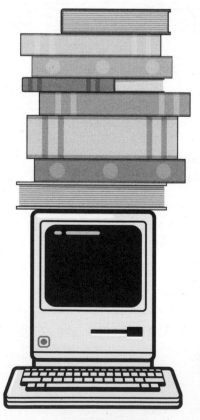

But, aside from that, tech wasn't really part of how I operated. If I was writing an essay and needed to research, I'd go to the library. Using an online search engine, whilst technically possible, just wasn't what people did. I suppose there must have been an early form of blogs back then, but we didn't consider what our peers thought to be particularly relevant. Everything we learned came from books written by academics and, as such, it was much harder to find diverse opinions from people of colour, women or anyone from a working-class background. Not impossible, of course, just more difficult.

Social media as we'd recognize it today didn't come into my life until much later, in the form of Myspace. Myspace was a primitive sort of Facebook. You had a profile, containing a finite number of pictures, some basic information and you could set it up to play a particular song when people clicked on it. There was also a chat function, but it was all a bit clunky and difficult to navigate. This didn't stop us going absolutely wild for it. I cannot tell you how many hours of my twenties I spent chatting nonsense on Myspace when I was supposed to be working (in my defence, I had a series of fist-chewingly boring jobs and some terrible bosses during this time).

In my late twenties, I moved to London, where everyone was raving about this new app called '**Twitter**'. At first, I resisted. I remember being really annoyed when I was trying to watch a TV show with my flatmates and they'd all be staring at their individual little screens rather than the communal big screen. It struck me as antisocial.

When they explained that they were 'following the hashtag' for whatever we were watching, I thought it sounded like a load of daft nonsense and simply could not fathom why anyone would want to spend their evenings that way. I recall vividly feeling this way and the disdain I had for people who'd start sentences with 'This person I follow on Twitter reckons . . .' Yet, as I type, I have not only indisputably *become* one of those people, I also can't really remember why I was so indignant about it.

That's a pretty conclusive example of how tech can fundamentally change your personality (see chapter 2).

By 2011, I was tweeting like a Trojan and in 2016 I had the somewhat dubious honour of being named by the BBC as one of the UK's most prolifically trolled people[1]. My name and photos were being shared in all manner of dubious, misogynistic forums in dark and relatively unexplored corners of the internet and I was receiving a tweet telling me to kill myself, or threatening me with violence, about once every three minutes. What had I done to provoke such ire? The short answer is: **I was a woman in the public eye with opinions**.

How did I deal with it? Well, first I tried drawing attention to it by screenshotting it and sharing it with my followers. This gave me the comfort and validation I was seeking, because, of course, lots of people got in touch to say how awful it was and that I didn't deserve it. But then I read a report by the Centre for Countering Digital Hate (their details are at the back of this book) which advised that the best way to deal with trolls is to block, report and ignore. This is for two reasons: firstly, because whilst 99% of your followers might think a troll's comment is despicable, 1% might be intrigued and that's how trolls grow their own followings. Secondly, because it might be triggering for people who follow you and have experience of the things the troll is targeting you for.

These days, I have really good filters, which means I don't see comments from trolls, even if I'm tagged, unless I search my own name. Sometimes, I find it quite illuminating to read through trolling comments. It helped me write this book, for example. There's a definite pattern to it and it absolutely says more about them than me. I do, however, have to be in the right headspace. I'd never search my name if I was feeling low or anxious.

If you go into the settings function on your social media, you'll see there are options there to automatically hide comments from accounts which are really new or have less than a certain number of followers. You can also mute certain keywords. There's more information on how to do this on the charity Glitch's website and again you can find details at the back of this book.

Today, I choose to use only three social media platforms: **Twitter** (because I'm a journalist and there's a strong argument to say I wouldn't be able to do my job without it), **Instagram** (because it is, in my experience at least, a fairly benign and supportive community, especially when compared with Twitter, which is a horrendous skipfire) and **WhatsApp** (see above re: my enduring love of texting). I'm not on Facebook because it's too annoying (I know you love your kids. I would assume that. Stop telling me) or TikTok/Snapchat, etc. because, frankly, I'm too old and they're not for me.

For the purposes of writing this book, I have talked to a lot of teens, as well as experts on the platforms I don't use, to fill in the gaps in my knowledge. I've also tried to focus on the universals – truths which apply to all social media platforms because they all operate on broadly the same business model and use similar manipulation techniques and **algorithms** (in maths, an algorithm is a set of instructions you can use to solve a particular problem). When used in relation to social media, however, we mean the way the app sorts what posts are in your feed and what information you see. They do this based on your past activity, but also on what is likely to hold your attention for the longest. We'll explore why that is a little later on.

I wanted you to know the role tech has played in my life because I think it puts me in a perfect position to write this book. I'm old enough to remember what life was like before the widespread dominance of the internet, but not so old that I find it bewildering. That's a perspective only a limited number of people have and, once my generation are dead, no one will ever have again. Which brings me to . . .

SOCIAL MEDIA AND YOU

There's a fable in which a scientist in the nineteenth century found **the best way to boil a frog** (don't worry, it didn't really happen. No actual frogs were harmed in this anecdote). In the fable, the scientist tries to put the frog into a pan of pre-boiled water and of course it jumps away, sensing that it is scalding hot. But then the scientist places the frog in a pan of tepid water and slowly, incrementally increases the temperature by a few degrees every minute. The frog doesn't notice the water gradually getting hotter, so (spoiler alert) remains there until it boils to death.

The reason this (again, I must emphasize, completely untrue) story is so often repeated is because it's a beautiful analogy for how the human mind works. People are, generally speaking, reticent to sudden change. Even if the change in question is positive, we would generally rather remain comfortably in a familiar situation. The best way to introduce change to a life, or a society, is gradually.

When it comes to the internet and social media, teenagers are the second frog. If you were born into a world of Wi-Fi, smartphones, tablets and instant access to internet, you have always been immersed in the water. You are less likely, therefore, to notice as it approaches boiling point.

This might explain why, when I ask people your age to list the causes of their stress and anxiety, social media usually comes fairly **near the bottom** of that list (and sometimes isn't mentioned at all). Teens will, however, frequently cite:

- **pressure to perform**
- **body image anxiety**
- **comparing themselves to their peers**
- **not having enough time in the day to do everything they need to do**

. . . All of which, as we will see, are problems exacerbated by technology.

Parents, on the other hand, often tend to **overestimate** the impact of technology. They generally see none of the advantages and worry that any time their child is near a screen it necessarily means they're being groomed/cyberbullied/radicalized when they could just as easily be reading *The Complete Works of Shakespeare* or watching a documentary about the plight of the rainforest. That's because parents are the first frog. Their childhoods likely involved little to no technology and the speed with which the world has changed is terrifying, from their perspective. Often, they project their own terror onto their children.

The truth, I suspect, is somewhere in between the perspectives of teenagers and their parents. The internet, like most things, is neither wholly brilliant nor completely evil and how it affects you depends to a large extent on how you use it. It's also indisputably here to stay. There's no point in us harking back to an age where people didn't walk around with their faces buried in their phones because those times are gone. It's far better to work out how we can deal with reality as it is.

After all: **ultimately, we're all boiling frogs.**

CHAPTER 1

UNDERSTANDING WHAT TECH DOES TO YOUR BRAIN

THE ATTENTION ECONOMY

Social media is, theoretically at least, completely **free** for us to use. Yet the tech companies which provide those platforms are worth **billions of dollars** and make millions more each year. The financial transactions which allow social media to exist are not between the platform and the user, but with organizations, brands, companies and individuals who pay the platform to ensure their content is seen by users. This is usually referred to as sponsored content, or sponcon.

Most of us know this. We're aware that social media companies make money through advertising. However, according to studies done by psychologists[2], most of us also believe we are not affected by the impact of advertising. We think we're far too clever, or maybe even just oblivious, to possibly have our beliefs or behaviours impacted by sponsored content.

And therein lies the problem, because really everything you need to know about how social media affects your brain depends upon you accepting that:

There are people and institutions out there trying (and, in many cases, succeeding) to influence how you think and feel.

Once you wrap your head around that, everything else makes sense.

The first and most important thing to understand is that we now live in what's known as 'the Attention Economy'. This means, in terms of how your average person lives day-to-day, the amount of money they physically **spend** is less relevant than the amount they **engage** with stuff – what they read, watch, click on and who they follow. Each day, millions of individuals and organizations use the internet to compete for our time and our clicks. The more of our engagement they can score, the more money they ultimately make.

Take an influencer, for example. The more followers they have and the more they are able to prove those followers actually watch, listen to and read what they have to say, the greater the chance they have of being able to persuade brands to sponsor them or give them free products. They will therefore devote themselves to ensuring they are creating content which grabs and then holds your attention.

That's a fairly benign example. As we will see, the quest to win our engagement gets a lot more sinister when we start to consider tech addiction and those with a political agenda.

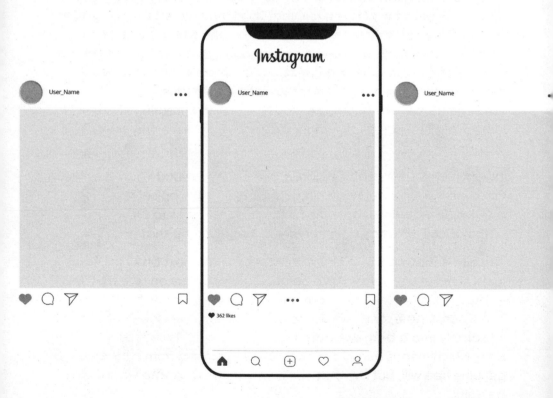

Vast amounts of skill and trickery are poured into ensuring we remain locked into technology for longer than we might have originally intended.

Take streaming services like Netflix, Amazon Prime and YouTube. Once we have finished watching one video, or one episode of a series, a related video, or the next episode, begins to play automatically. We have to intervene in order to stop that process.

The aim is that we will think the thumbnail of the next bit of content looks sufficiently interesting to be persuaded to stay on and watch it. Thus, a plan to take a look at one video can become a deep dive into a **scroll hole**, or a promise to only watch one episode can lead inexorably into a **binge watch**. Tech is always trying to steal our time, which means our habits are not being formed from a place of genuine free will, but by what our Tech Overlords dictate we should be doing.

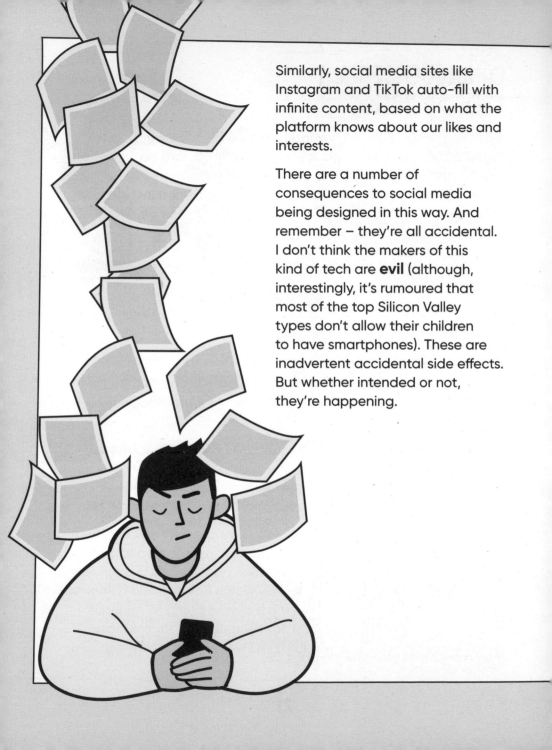

Similarly, social media sites like Instagram and TikTok auto-fill with infinite content, based on what the platform knows about our likes and interests.

There are a number of consequences to social media being designed in this way. And remember – they're all accidental. I don't think the makers of this kind of tech are **evil** (although, interestingly, it's rumoured that most of the top Silicon Valley types don't allow their children to have smartphones). These are inadvertent accidental side effects. But whether intended or not, they're happening.

CONSEQUENCE NO. 1
TECH ADDICTION

Addictive behaviours are ultimately guided by a neurotransmitter called dopamine. Dopamine is released in the reward centres of our brains when we are engaging in pleasurable behaviours which make us feel good. This can be anything from eating something tasty, to listening to music or creating art. It doesn't have to be a 'bad' activity.

Over time, this can train our brains to be wired towards seeking out **pleasure** and avoiding anything we find **dull** or uncomfortable. This is a problem in so far as life unfortunately involves at least 50% dull and uncomfortable things and if you avoid them, there's consequences for your health, grades and stress levels (see 'social media becomes stressful' on page 29).

LOGGING ON TO A SOCIAL MEDIA APP RELEASES

DOPAMINE

SIGNALS IN THE BRAIN.

Everything from the colours used to the feeling of 'pushing a button' or 'refreshing your feed' (when actually you're just touching a piece of glass) is designed to stimulate dopamine production. Notifications and the 'pull to refresh' feature (when we drag our finger down the screen and our feeds auto-fill with more content) are also based on the same principles which make gambling so addictive.

Think of it like those slot machines you get in casinos. You pull a lever which prompts three wheels with various pictures to spin. If you get a match of three lemons (for example), you win. But it could land on any number of other possible combinations, which makes the process unpredictable and exciting. Statistically, it's unlikely you'll get three lemons, but every so often it will fall on that combination. It's the not knowing that makes it so compelling and, ultimately, addictive.

Whenever we refresh our feeds, we don't know what we're going to see, but we're **hoping** for likes and affirmation. If we got likes and positive comments every time we refreshed, that would eventually become boring. But we don't, so we start compulsively refreshing in pursuit of the good stuff but also addicted to the uncertainty of what might appear in our feed, each time.

Ultimately, that's led to a situation where the average person spends four hours on social media, checking their phone anything between 85 and 200 times per day, depending on which study you read.[3].

THAT'S A QUARTER OF OUR WAKING LIFETIMES.

It's the reason you bump into people or nearly get run over, because your face is buried in your phone. It's the reason we half-watch movies, or half-listen to conversations, scrolling with one hand.

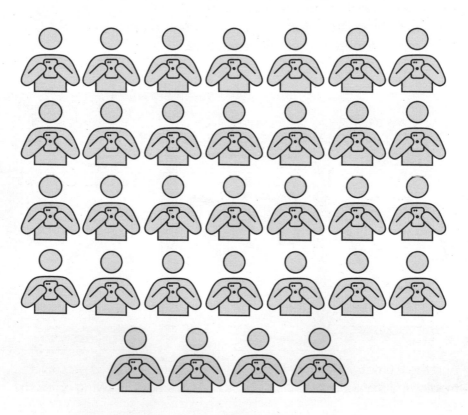

And the ultimate question to ask is – if half our attention is on social media and the other on the rest of life, are we really enjoying any of it?

EXPERT TAKE

'Social media is this perfect storm, mixing two highly desirable things together and one of them is validation – which is not the same as recognition, the thing we truly need – and this kind of fruit machine effect of how notifications work on social media – the unexpected and random reward system. When you mix those two together, it's like psychological crack . . . Your reward system rewards you for just getting a notification, but if the notification is about you there's a kind of ego gratification that goes alongside it.

'You can make a comparison to junk food. Junk food is really moreish because it satisfies our basic needs – it's either salty or sugary or fatty. But it's not good to consume these things in massive quantities. You want more because it's pleasurable but it also misses the psychological nourishment of real relationships.'

Dr Aaron Balick, author of The Psychodynamics of Social Networking

CONSEQUENCE NO. 2
SOCIAL MEDIA BECOMES STRESSFUL

Playing a video game is a perfectly legitimate way to unwind and decompress after a difficult day at school/college/uni/work. It's creative, it involves problem-solving, hand-eye coordination and, if you're playing a multiplayer game, socializing. Yet most of the parents I speak to don't see it this way. In fact, they tell me they spend what seems like hours trying to prise their offspring off their damned Xboxes and are always met with the response:

'I just have to finish this leeeeeeveeeeeel!'

Why do you have to finish the level? The answer is twofold – firstly, because you'll get a sense of satisfaction and accomplishment, but secondly, because most games only allow you to save your progress, or bank your points, once you have reached a certain point. It's not like a book, where you can stick a slip of paper in to remind you where you're up to so you can come back to it at a later point. I'm sure the game makers could design it that way, but the way games are designed generally involves a bigger investment of time over and above what we might have intended, or what would be ideal – and that's great for them.

Thus, an intention to spend thirty minutes having a quick game before you start your homework (fine) has become a four-hour marathon session, leaving no time to do your homework (stressful).

Tech addiction isn't just about the impact it's having on our brains, it's about what it's doing to our quality of life. Social media and gaming should be a hobby, like sport or playing the violin. You wouldn't break off a conversation halfway through to quickly play a few notes on your violin, or leave the dinner table in the middle of a meal to kick a football in a net. And yet, somehow, tech is permeating every aspect of our lives and stealing far more of our time than most of us realize.

WHAT TO DO IF TECH IS STEALING YOUR TIME

Viktor E. Frankl[4], an Austrian neuroscientist, once said:

'Between stimulus and response there is a space.
In that space is our power to choose our response.
In our response lies our growth and our freedom.'

The trick, I think, is to

expand

that moment between stimulus, i.e. the urge to do something, and response – doing it.

In order to do this, we first have to **notice** and then, if possible, **expand** that space between stimulus and response. Tech is designed to stimulate us. And if we just react in whatever way the tech is telling us to, we're nothing more than an extension of an algorithm. But if we consciously choose when we want to use tech, and for how long, then we are in charge.

Say you've decided you'd like to spend thirty minutes scrolling through Instagram, or uploading content to TikTok – set an alarm for half an hour's time. If it's on your phone, it might be enough to jolt you out of your reverie. If you can get an old-fashioned alarm clock or wind-up kitchen timer and place it a long way away from you – ideally in a different room – then you'll have to find the alarm to switch it off when it starts screeching. It's at this point you can have a conversation with yourself. Ask yourself:

What else do I have to do today?

If I carry on messing around with tech, will I have enough time to do those things?

If the answer to the second question is 'no', then continuing to play the game, or spend time on socials, is going to add to your stress. That's the very definition of ironic, considering it's meant to be a 'fun' pastime which reduces the amount of stress you experience. The key is to catch yourself before whatever it is you're doing tumbles over the tipping point between stress release and stressful and to be confident enough in your own decisions to know the best thing to do is to break away before that happens.

CONSEQUENCE NO. 3
POLARIZATION OF OPINION

When we create a social media account, we voluntarily give the internet quite a lot of personal information about ourselves. We tell it where we live, approximately what age bracket we fit into, our gender and – by dint of who we follow and what we engage with – what we're into. This is all measured by an algorithm whose job it is to establish what type of person you are, anticipate your interests and project content into your feed based on these estimates.

In the terms and conditions (which no one ever reads), it says that your social media accounts can access your **camera** and your **microphone**. You can disable these functions manually, but that would prohibit you from being able to load video and photo content to the site, or from sending a voice note. That's what the site needs access to your camera and microphone for – to fulfil its own basic functions.

However, that access isn't limited to when you're actually using a platform. In theory, the site's algorithms can access your photos or listen in to your conversations

AGREE

WHENEVER THEY LIKE.

And when I say 'listen in to your conversations', I don't mean only the actual chats you have using your actual phone – I mean **anything you're saying near your phone**. That's why if you consistently talk about a brand or type of product within 'earshot' of your phone you will start to see adverts for those products appear in your feed. Or if you consistently express an interest in something – a place, or a type of animal, for example – your feed will start to include content featuring those things.

In addition to this, there are cookies. We all click the 'this website uses cookies' button without thinking twice because pop-ups are annoying, time is finite and we're desperate to buy those shoes/see that video of a hamster eating an aubergine. Yet with just that one click, you're enabling up to fifty organizations to access your information[5]. The website you are visiting, plus their affiliated organizations, then know everything on your social media profiles, plus other activities you take part in on the World Wide Web.

Ultimately, there are many complex algorithms sharing information about you all the time behind the scenes. Or behind the screens, if you will (see what I did there). Social media sites collect this data/information in order to build a comprehensive profile of the kind of person you are.

SO, WHAT'S THE PROBLEM WITH THIS?

Doesn't it just mean that you end up being exposed only to things you have pre-existing interests in?

YES . . . AND THAT IN ITSELF *IS* THE PROBLEM.

People with similar tastes in entertainment, food, hobbies, etc. also tend to have a significant overlap in their socio-political opinions. So, if you're vegan, for example – the chances are you also have an interest in saving the planet and the environment. That means you'll instinctively tend to dislike politicians or parties who deny climate change is an issue. These politicians and parties tend to fall on the right of the political spectrum. So, just by looking up recipes for vegan brownies, you could end up in a slipstream of people with left-wing sensibilities.

Imran Ahmed, who is CEO of the Centre for Countering Digital Hate, asks us to imagine these slipstreams like colours. Let's say, having evaluated your musical tastes, fashion choices, hobbies and habits, food and entertainment preferences, social media has decided you're a 'green' person. You're now in a slipstream of other 'green' people with similar interests and views of the world. In your green slipstream, you are constantly having your own biases affirmed. No one ever disagrees with your opinions, because all the green people think in broadly the same way. Therefore, you might begin to think, 'I am right! I am totally right about everything! I literally never encounter anyone who disagrees with my point of view! Maybe I am a genius with the solutions to all that is wrong in the world!'.

However, if you could zoom out and see social media in its entirety, it would look like a kaleidoscope. There are slipstreams of every imaginable hue – red, purple, blue, violet, orange, yellow, turquoise and magenta. And all the people in those slipstreams are also having their opinions affirmed.

You know when you encounter a person who believes something really 'out there' like the world is flat, or the King is really a lizard, or Trump was a feminist? You think to yourself 'how on Earth did this person end up so stupid?'. But they're not necessarily stupid, they have just been immersed in their slipstream for so long that their reality has shifted.

Similarly, people rarely have civilized conversations online. This is particularly true of the comments sections underneath YouTube videos and newspaper articles and it is *super* true of Twitter.

In fact, most conversations on Twitter seem ultimately to end with one party accusing the other of either being a Nazi or a snowflake. Which, whilst entertaining, is not conducive to genuinely effective discourse.

HUMANITY HAS TO HAVE SOME AGREED, CENTRALIZED TRUTHS, OTHERWISE WE'RE SCREWED.

We can't all just walk around with our own metaphorical virtual reality headsets on, experiencing a world which looks the way we think it should, however tempting that might sound. Compromise, collaboration and communication are key to the future of human beings. They're necessary for huge, global projects like peace. But they're also essential on a micro level – at some point in your career or personal life it's going to be necessary for you to relate to, empathize and get on with someone whose beliefs, prejudices and biases are different from your own.

It's therefore absolutely imperative to venture outside of your slipstream. Later in this book we'll look at online role models and how to tell the difference between a person who is making a legitimate point which you disagree with and someone who is just trying to make you angry for clicks. Having a handful of the former in your feed is essential social media practice.

CONSEQUENCE NO. 4
RADICALIZATION

When you are streaming, the service will suggest a next piece of content which has similar themes to what you have searched for. It will also be slightly more dramatic in its nature and will therefore continue to engage you.

Let's say you are on TikTok watching a video of a kitten. The next video it suggests might be a video of a kitten on a trampoline. Then the next video might be several kittens on a trampoline, bouncing into one another adorably. Since each video is a little bit more exciting, you remain hooked. The most obvious example of this strategy is on porn sites (see below).

Cute kitten small cat using trampoline

Similarly, tech designed to steal our time and keep our engagement can inadvertently lead to radicalization of political opinions. Let's say, for example, a twelve-year-old boy is curious about feminism and wants to learn more about what it actually is. He types 'what is feminism?' into YouTube and the site provides the most relevant result – a feminist giving a basic description of what the word means (equality for all, regardless of gender). But, after that, the algorithm is no longer concerned with relevance, its job is to provide something more shocking and therefore more engaging. It won't be long before that twelve-year-old ends up on a video of some alt-right guy ranting from his mum's basement (we've all seen them) about how men are the new disadvantaged underclass and feminism is a cancer which must be eradicated. This isn't just an arbitrary example, there's evidence of boys as young as twelve being inducted into the so-called 'manosphere' (the corner of the internet where truly horrific misogyny, racism and homophobia live) this way. See Laura Bates's excellent (if disturbing) book *Men Who Hate Women* for more info on this. The best way to arm yourself against falling down this type of toxic rabbit hole is to search fresh each time you want to find something. To clarify, search engines, social media and more traditional websites all use these types of algorithms and they all communicate with one another. So, if you're watching a video or reading an article online and you find you have questions, or want to find out more about a particular aspect of what has been written or said, type that into the search bar rather than just clicking on the next thing the site suggests.

PORNOGRAPHY

Eeek! We're going to have to talk about this, because it's *everywhere* online and even if you have zero interest in seeking it out yourself, the chances are you are going to stumble upon it. You might have been shown porn by another person at school, or have been searching for something else and had it suddenly appear in your feed. Whatever the reason, statistics show that by the time you reach sixteen, there's a 97% chance you will have seen it.

It's normal to be curious about sex, especially before you've actually done it. But it's also super important to realize that pornography is created for entertainment. Actual sexual experiences are – and indeed should be – very different.

The first reason for this is that, for a porn actor, having sex is their job. They're not doing it for their own pleasure, they're trying to appeal to the viewer. That isn't how sex usually works. You wouldn't watch a video of a professional dancer doing an incredibly complex and acrobatic dance routine and then expect to be able to do it yourself. You also know that professional dancer probably wouldn't do that routine if they were just dancing socially in a club, or at a wedding. It's kind of the same principle.

The second reason is that porn is the most obvious example of algorithms not only trying to guess, but also actually shaping our preferences.

Pornographic content is embedded with keywords. So, let's say you click on a video which features a person with blonde hair, this will be noted by the algorithm, which will go on to suggest videos featuring other blonde-haired people. However, it will also suggest content which is slightly more explicit and 'hardcore' than the last thing you watched. Just like with all streaming services, it's trying to keep you watching for as long as possible.

Remember: the algorithm doesn't care *WHY* you are watching, just

THAT you are. Content which is shocking tends to grab people's attention. Often, they don't even find it enjoyable, they're just completely grossed out and can't look away. What that means is you're likely to be witnessing sexual acts online it would have taken a person years to learn about, pre-internet.

Experts believe this can lead to 'sexual extremism' – especially in people who watch porn regularly. Their expectations of what sex should be, what their partner should feel comfortable doing and how they should look, have been massively skewed by what they have seen online [6]

This is a particular issue for people of your age. It's difficult enough trying to deal with the hormonal rollercoaster that is being a teenager without worrying that you don't look like a Barbie/Action Man with your clothes off. You might also be making your first tentative forays into sexual experiences like kissing and touching (it's also totally normal if you're not – there's no such thing as 'the right time', as long as you and whoever you're doing it with feel ready and are able to consent). It's these kinds of experiences which, gradually, begin to teach you what you do and don't like and help build your confidence.

But please don't let porn be your guide as to what you should be doing, sexually. It's the equivalent of learning your lessons about love from Disney movies (my generation did that and it didn't end well when we eventually realized the path to romance did not involve singing to woodland creatures whilst having a waist the same width as our necks).

Having said all that, not all pornography is the same. The more 'mainstream' sites tend to have the kind of content I describe above and it's generally all a bit grubby and unhealthy for everyone involved. However, there are also sites which strive to make more ethical pornographic content, where consent is at the heart of everything and all the bodies are diverse and realistic. If you were intent on looking at porn anyway, they are a much better option.

SUMMARY

Technology isn't actively trying to turn us into a load of shouty, self-entitled, sexually-confused idiots but, nonetheless, that is what it is achieving. Its imperatives are commercial –

ALL IT WANTS IS FOR US TO STAY ONLINE LONGER SO MORE MONEY CAN BE MADE.

That is a neutral aim, but one that has moral implications.

The internet is therefore nothing like a textbook or an encyclopaedia. It's not like all the info is just there, collated by experts, waiting for us to look it up. Everything we see, hear or experience online has been tailored to our perceived preconceptions. **Imagine if, when you were studying at school, everyone got their own textbook with different information, based on what they thought was already true**. No one's passing their exams that way.

Being wise to this – and the potential impact it can have on how we think and behave – is the first and most important step towards fighting it.

CHAPTER 2

EVALUATING ARGUMENTS, SPOTTING FAKE NEWS AND COMING UP WITH YOUR 'TAKE'

In March 2021, the *Byline Times* (a left-leaning newspaper) published a piece called 'Home Office Fails to Explain Strange Expenses'[7]. The article was thoroughly fact-checked and included a list of payments made from the Home Office's 'procurement card', amounting to hundreds of thousands of pounds, to companies including one that makes cupcakes, an electronics store in Alabama and a diet consultant. The payment that caught everyone's attention, though, was £77,269.40 to a company called 'SP Beautiful Brows'.

NEWSPAPER HEADLINE

The story was picked up by other left-wing outlets, less scrupulous than the *Byline Times*, who printed the £77K figure without context, suggesting it had all been spent on Priti Patel's eyebrows (who was the Home Secretary and therefore in charge of the Home Office). Several 'takes' emerged on social media, including things like 'no money for refugees but £77K for the Home Secretary's eyebrows'. As a result, 'Priti Patel's Eyebrows' trended on Twitter for forty-eight hours.

I, thinking I was being hilarious, took to Google and searched 'world's most expensive eyebrows'. I found a picture of a model with jewels stuck to her brow bone and tweeted it with the caption 'Trying to figure out what £77K worth of eyebrows looks like **#PritiPatel**'. It got a couple of hundred likes and I logged off, satisfied my social media work for the day was done.

The next morning, I received a private message from a journalist working for a right-wing tabloid. It said:

> **'Hi Natasha, I am writing a story for tomorrow's [redacted] about false claims that Priti Patel spent £77K getting her eyebrows done. The "story" appears to be fake news. The Home Office has made it clear that the expenditure was on PPE*, including hand sanitizer. I noticed you tweeting about the story. Do you accept that it is false? Is this not an example of how fake news spreads online? Do you regret sharing the story and will you now apologize for doing so?'**

I never replied to that message (because I considered it rude and knew they'd print whatever I said in reply in a way that portrayed me unfavourably), but I did have a long think about whether I did, indeed, 'regret sharing the story'. And it turns out I do, but not necessarily for the reasons the journalist might have assumed.

I saw a social media bandwagon and jumped on it, for LOLs and a bit of engagement. I didn't seriously think the Home Secretary had spent £77K getting her eyebrows done. It was a joke, and I thought everyone who saw it would receive it as such. I didn't seriously expect anyone to look at my tweet and think 'Natasha Devon has heavily implied that the Home Secretary's eyebrows are made of rubies and diamonds, purchased at the taxpayer's expense, and therefore it must be true! I won't be voting for her party again!'.

What my actions did do, however, was enable the right-wing tabloid to present the original story in the *Byline Times* as completely false. Which, of course, it wasn't (ironically, that was the real fake news). There might have been an

---

* *'Personal Protective Equipment' . . . Or 'Priti Patel's Eyebrows'* ☺

44

explanation for the £77K given to an eyebrow company which apparently also makes hand sanitizer, but there were twelve other unexplained 'expenses' in the article, which the Home Office were able to **totally ignore** because the eyebrow joke had trended. That story pretty much encapsulates what I want to discuss later on in this chapter. When we share fake news, we might do it knowingly because it's funny, or cute, but the cumulative impact is often to reduce an important story to a silly, tribal battle. But, first, I want to explore how fake news starts, who spreads it and why it can be a very effective (and scary, in the wrong hands) social media tool.

WHAT IS FAKE NEWS?

For the purposes of this chapter, the term 'fake news' encompasses any post which contains deliberately misleading information in order to encourage social media users to purchase a particular product, join a group, buy into an ideology or behave in a certain way (e.g. change their voting intention). Ultimately, however, the aim of fake news is that it is shared as many times as possible.

Fake news is often deliberately designed to play into our existing fears/prejudices and/or confirm some of our irrational beliefs about the world and it is often targeted specifically at the people most likely to fall for it. For this reason, people often do not take the trouble to check fake news before sharing it, because it seems like it should be right, or because it has been shared by another person they trust. That's how, in the words of my LBC colleague James O'Brien[8]

'fake news can be halfway round the world before the truth has got its trousers on.'

The consequences of fake news are broadly twofold:

1 People fall down a rabbit hole of disinformation, which begins quite plausibly ('everyone you know is voting for this candidate, so why did their rival win the election?') and slowly radicalizes them into something utterly implausible ('it's because their rival is part of a cabal of lizards wearing human skins who drink the blood of kidnapped children!').

2 If a piece of fake news takes off, there ends up being so many people who believe it that they have to be acknowledged in more mainstream reporting, because they are a story in and of themselves. This inadvertently adds legitimacy to a theory which was originally pulled out of a nefarious person's arse because people think 'there must be some truth to it if this many people believe it' (e.g. climate change denial).

WHO FALLS FOR FAKE NEWS?

According to Marianna Spring[9] a specialist disinformation and social media reporter at the BBC, contrary to popular belief there is no 'profile' for the sort of person who might fall for fake news. Rather, there are certain forms of fake news that certain people are more likely to believe depending on factors such as their age group and which forms of tech they favour.

Older people are more likely to fall for phishing emails and to click on dodgy links claiming to be from their 'bank'.

People in their **thirties and forties** are most likely to believe something sent to them via WhatsApp from someone they're friends with or related to.

Teenagers mainly get their fake news from YouTube, or from trusted influencers on TikTok or Instagram.

In all three of these examples, we can see that it's less about the content itself and more about the perceived reliability of who it has come from. This is dangerous because, as we will see in the next chapter, no one is infallible, or right 100% of the time.

WHO IS CREATING AND SHARING THE NEWS?

Bearing in mind that who news *comes from* is more important, in many regards, than what it actually *is*, be sure to ask yourself some questions about the source of the potential fakery:

WHAT IS THEIR EXPERTISE?

It's important to be really shrewd on this, for three reasons:

1. **Social media removes social cues.**

If I came into your school, college or university, I would be in your territory. If I wanted to know what it was like being a young person in, say, Peterborough and you happened to be a young person living in Peterborough, you would be more of an expert on that topic than me, who is not a young person from Peterborough. So, if I came to your school specifically to talk to you about being a young person in Peterborough, I would, naturally and without thinking about it, show deference to you during that conversation and let you lead it.

On the internet, however, all those geographical and contextual factors are removed. Everyone's opinion is, at least theoretically, worth the same as everyone else's. You could therefore do a TikTok video giving your perspective on what it is like to be a young person in Peterborough, I could do the same and the perspective that is given the most credence is whoever's gets the most views. Which is not only very undemocratic, it is also not the best way to obtain quality intel.

Similarly, the people with the most reach and therefore the loudest voices on social media are those with the most followers, but they're not necessarily the most correct, or the people most scrupulously verifying their content. For example, cast members of reality TV shows often have followings amounting to several million, but if you've ever watched reality TV, you'll understand why I say it's important not to get all of your political and/or scientific information from its stars.

2. Lots of people are called 'experts' and they are . . . but not in the thing they're discussing.

When the COVID pandemic first struck in the UK in 2020, lots of 'experts' were wading in to give their opinion. Those which matched the political motivations of certain media outlets/political groups were amplified. On closer inspection, however, their qualifications were in areas which were not relevant to knowing anything about the best way to handle a pandemic.

EXPERT ON THE DANGERS OF TRAMPOLINES

DR WHISKERS

If someone has a PhD in Greek mythology, they're supremely qualified to talk about Greek mythology. However, just because they have 'Dr' before their name (as anyone with a PhD does), it doesn't necessarily mean they know anything about medicine/ viruses/disease control.

Lots of people seem impressively qualified at a glance, but a quick look at their official university profile/Wiki page or similar will tell you how relevant their experience and expertise is to the topic they are opining on.

That's not to say their opinion automatically has no value. Merely that if we are discussing, say, COVID-19, all opinions are less valid than a virologist's.

3. Real experts tend not to have pithy/shareable opinions.

I've learned this from interviewing many, many genuine experts on my radio show. Real experts know how nuanced all issues tend to be and are confident enough in the depth of their knowledge to say when they don't know something for sure.

In fact, what I've found is that actual experts are more likely to say 'evidence on that isn't yet clear' or 'it's a bit more complicated than that, in fact . . .' or even 'I don't know' than to blag it. This makes them more honest, but less useful for social media fodder. Be honest, if it came to a choice between watching a ten-minute video of a person saying, 'I can only go by what the evidence is telling us so far and that is fairly complicated, but I'll try to summarize it for you in layman's terms . . .' or a thirty-second clip of a person shouting:

'I HAVE THE SOLUTION TO EVERYTHING AND IT'S VERY SIMPLE!'

which one would you be more likely to go for?

EXPERT TAKE

'Look at what people are selling. If they are selling you a solution to a problem that they are themselves discussing in a lot of detail, that's potentially a red flag. If they're telling you "this is a problem and by the way here is me selling you the solution in the form of a supplement" or something like that, then ask yourself whether they conveniently invented the problem after they found the solution.

'Also, if something makes you feel afraid, then that person probably isn't the best person to be looking to for your information because fear is largely unnecessary and unhelpful with health. Ideally, messaging should be encouraging, supportive, nuanced and should not make you afraid. Especially when it comes to food – fear is unnecessary.'

Pixie Turner, nutritionist (MSc) (RNutr)

THE PROBLEM WITH CHECKING SUSPECTED FAKE NEWS AGAINST 'TRADITIONAL MEDIA'

When I interviewed a representative from charity Childnet, whose mission it is to make the internet safe for children and young people, they told me teenagers will usually cross-check something they see on social media on 'traditional media' sites (newspapers, TV, radio) if they suspect it might be fake news.

Whilst there are some rules traditional media have to follow about checking sources and impartiality, some are more stringent than others in terms of following them. In fact, when it comes to the tabloid press, they're quite likely to have a 'print some total hokum now and apologize in tiny letters on page 47 tomorrow' type attitude (read James Felton's brilliant book *Sunburn: The Unofficial History of the Sun in 99 Headlines* for numerous examples of this). It's therefore not as simple as believing that if a story is verifiable in traditional media, it must necessarily be true.

Furthermore, we often think social media discussions are dictated by what is printed, or said, in traditional media, but it also works the other way around. How often have you heard a newsreader say, 'The Prime Minister has tweeted today . . .' or read a salacious story in a magazine about an Insta war between two reality TV contestants?

On TV and radio, they're also usually trying to create content which is going to get lots of engagement when they clip it up and post it to social media. This will often involve asking people with the most 'outrageous' opinions to appear on their shows, regardless of whether those opinions are a product of evidence-based reality. Again, not all programmes do this, but just because you see a clip of a person in a suit saying something on a recognizable media platform doesn't mean they're necessarily speaking truth.

Then, of course, there is clickbait: with millions of pieces of content vying for your attention, media companies have to

TRAMPOLINES ARE EVIL
And so is anyone who doesn't believe us

make sure their headlines are as intriguing as possible in order to make sure you choose to click through onto theirs. This often means the headlines you see bear little or no relevance to the pieces themselves. This process of oversimplification is not only very annoying for the people who produce the content (as a writer, I have no control whatsoever over the headlines put at the top of my articles. That doesn't, however, prevent people from shouting at me about them online), it's also dangerous because it means our feeds are populated with inflammatory and reductionist comments, which we subconsciously absorb. Whenever you're part of a conversation where someone says, 'I'm sure I read/heard somewhere that . . .' but they cannot remember the specific details, the chances are they saw a piece of clickbait, their brain remembered it because it was alarmist or entertaining, but it actually has a very loose relationship with the facts.

On top of this, there are also blogs which are designed stylistically to look like online newspapers. They put a newspaper-type crest at the top and call it something like 'The Daily Real Expose of Truth'. Whilst newspapers (particularly tabloids) are very far from perfect in terms of their reporting, they do at least have to follow some legal guidelines (or get sued). Blogs aren't subject to the same restrictions.

As a side note here, I've noticed people are more likely to believe YouTubers or other video-based influencers if their main schtick is pointing out agendas or inaccuracies in other forms of media. Just because someone can see that the media often deliberately skews events to provoke strong emotions in their audiences (and, let's face it, just about everyone can see that because it's really obvious) doesn't mean that everything else they say is 100% true. Neither does it mean that there's a global conspiracy 'mainstream media' agenda to 'take them down' when they're criticised, or exposed for talking out of their bums.

BETTER WAYS TO CROSS-CHECK SUSPECTED FAKE NEWS

As well as thinking about the motivations and expertise of the person sharing, it's worth doing the following:

1

Ask yourself what the end goal is. In particular, if a news story is being used to sell you something, beware. This is, according to nutritionist Pixie Turner a tactic often used by so-called 'health influencers'. They create a scare story about a particular foodstuff in order to sell you a 'healthier' alternative. The Centre for Countering Digital Hate also produced a report in 2020[10] which showed how almost all anti-vax information on the web can be tracked back to a small group of wealthy people making enormous amounts of cash selling natural 'alternatives' to vaccines.

2

Reverse image search. Often, people claim an image 'proves' the point they're making. By simply reverse searching the image, you can find out if it's, for example, a stock photo they've ripped off Google, if it's been used elsewhere and, if you're lucky, when the picture was originally taken and where.

3

Seek out websites with a proven track-record of impartiality. For example, if the suspected fake news relates to health, have a look at what the NHS website has to say. BBC articles are also pretty good (when I worked with BBC Bitesize[11] to do some mental health content, they had what I was saying reviewed by numerous properly qualified doctor-type people).

4

Use fact-check websites. For example, fullfact.org publishes lists of misinformation doing the rounds on trending topics, such as the Russia/Ukraine War, climate change and vaccines, and explains why they're wrong. Be careful, though, as anyone can theoretically set up a website called something like TheActualTruthAboutStuff.com In 2019 the Conservative party famously changed their Twitter name and avatar to make it look like a fact-checking service during a televised leaders' debate[12].

5

Look at source material. This is probably the best way to check the truthfulness of suspected fake news, but it's also the most time-consuming and potentially boring. Most videos, posts and articles wishing to spread fake news will cite 'studies' which 'prove' their theories. Sometimes, they provide a link to these 'studies', or, if not, you can google them. You can then go back to the steps above and have a look at who wrote the study. You can also see whether it has a good sample size, if it's peer- reviewed and if it's been commissioned by someone likely to not be impartial (for example, by a company selling an alternative to what the study 'proves' is dangerous).

ARE YOU RESPONSIBLE FOR SPREADING FAKE NEWS?

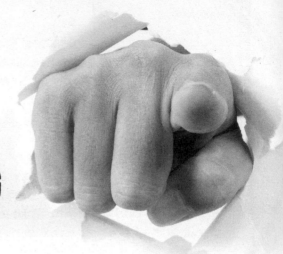

Posting something to social media is, technically, a form of 'publishing' and we are each responsible for our own content.

Barrister Daniel Barnett[18] says: 'Anything you post about any person or company has to be true, or at least be a fair opinion based on true facts, or they could sue you for defamation. In real life, that's not likely to happen unless you're wealthy and have got the money to pay them compensation and legal costs, but you still shouldn't libel someone.

'It's a criminal offence to post something that is grossly offensive or indecent. That can cover hate speech, revenge porn or racist comments. Less well known is that it's a criminal offence to post something which you know isn't true, which you're posting for the purpose of causing anxiety or annoyance, although anything clearly intended as a joke would not be caught by this.'

Looks like I'm safe on the jewelled eyebrows image, then.

EXPERT TAKE

'I spend a lot of time talking about how fake news causes real-world harm, so, for example, people who have lost their lives [through believing dangerous health advice they see online] or had their relationships ruined by very extreme conspiracy theories. But some fake news can actually be quite funny. It can generate a lot of likes. I have interviewed people who spread it who say "it was just really cool to have my post go viral".

'The problem is that it sets the wrong kind of precedent. It means that people think that it's okay to spread things that are untrue and that it doesn't have consequences, whereas in fact a lot of stuff, even if it is a joke, can have consequences.'

Marianna Spring, award-winning specialist reporter
on disinformation and social media

COMING UP WITH YOUR 'TAKE'

In her brilliant book *Outraged: Why Everyone's Shouting and No One is Talking*, Ashley 'Dotty' Charles says we should see our outrage as currency. Imagine all the **ducks*** you have to give are stored in one place, like savings in a bank account. Every time you feel sufficiently moved to comment on a story, you are 'spending' some of those ducks. It's therefore wise, Charles argues, to establish early what you're really passionate about and only spend your ducks generating outrage around these issues.

This will also help you to establish your 'brand'. People will see the themes in what you post and defer to you if they want to see a refreshing take on the particular topics you're known for.

The most compelling takes are:

☐ **• Original**

Don't just copy and paste what someone else has already said. If you can't think of something original to say, sit this one out.

---

* I want this book to be in libraries, so I'm not allowed to swear. I have therefore substituted the word I wanted to use for the word 'ducks', like predictive text on smartphones does all the time.

• Based on personal experience

If you have something directly relevant to the topic that's happened to you, people will appreciate you sharing it. Be wary of looking like you're trying to steal the limelight, however. This is particularly true if the story is about a marginalized community and you are not part of that community. Saying 'oh yeah, I know what it's like to be a persecuted Muslim because once this person said they didn't like my hat' is just going to make people angry.

• Funny

Unless there is absolutely no room for mickey-takage (e.g. terrorism, genocide, etc.), being funny gets you far on social media. Take a look at *The Poke*, who collect some of the most outrageously funny commentary on the web and compile them into handy streams, to see the type of thing I'm talking about.

• Authentic

This really goes back to the outrage and spending of ducks point I made earlier. I absolutely DETEST with all my being the term 'virtue signalling' (because it's often used to derail important conversations about equality), but I also think there are times when it can be used legitimately. It's really easy to spot when someone is just posting for clout, without fully understanding the story or the struggle behind it.

If you want to show that you care or are an ally but aren't fully across an issue, it's better to share content from, or signpost to, someone you follow and trust who is fully immersed and express solidarity with them (we'll talk about allyship later in this book).

Don't feel like you have to be 100% critical or gushing about something, either. You might find that this means you don't have anything original to say at all or you might find you come up with a genuine take a lot of people relate to when you say something like, 'I wanted to love/hate (such and such that everyone is raving about/criticizing) but actually here are the things I didn't appreciate/appreciated about it . . .'

You don't have to be really clever, either. One of my most shared posts is when I wrote 'ANSWER THE FRIGGIIIING QUEEEEESSSSSTIIIIIIIIIIIONNN!' during a Prime Minister's Questions in which the Prime Minister was staunchly dodging everything he was being asked (which is all politicians tbf). That was genuinely how I (and a lot of people) felt at the time.

CONCLUSION

There's a great podcast I listen to called *Standard Issue*[13], in which three very funny feminists called Hannah, Mickey and Jen dissect the week's news. In one episode, Hannah says:

'IF YOU'RE NOT SURE WHETHER YOU SHOULD POST SOMETHING, IT PROBABLY MEANS YOU SHOULDN'T.'

THAT'S THE BEST ADVICE, EVER.

CHAPTER 3

CHOOSING AND GETTING THE BEST FROM ONLINE ROLE MODELS

'Who'd be a teenager now?' is an expression I hear a lot. When asked to elaborate, the adult speaking usually says something along the lines of . . .

'Well, of course, we had exam stress, bullies, friendship issues, hormones, heartbreak and fashion disasters to deal with, too, but at least they weren't all captured on the internet where they created an indelible footprint and, even if deleted, could theoretically be found by anyone, for ever.'

As a side note, here, I'd like to say I'm not totally sold on these 'never take a selfie downing a shot of tequila with your knickers on your head because your employers might find it in ten years' time' type arguments. In an ideal world, one should always be as shrewd as possible and endeavour not to post anything online which one wouldn't wish one's mum to see. In reality, however, that isn't always a practical or viable strategy.

Most of us have *something* out there in the vastness of infinite cyberspace which, with the benefit of hindsight, we have realized doesn't portray us in our best light. If employers are going to discriminate based on those types of criteria, they'll find, particularly as the current cohort of teens enter the job market, that they have a tiny, almost non-existent, pool of candidates to choose from.

Plus, when it comes to nudity/sexual content, many of the people who have 'compromising' shots or footage of themselves online have been subjected to so-called 'revenge porn', which means, if they were refused employment on that basis, they would be being punished for being victims of a crime. And that's incredibly morally dubious.

But this is a rant for another time . . .

Whilst social media is constantly demonized by people claiming it is responsible for all the woes they imagine befall 'the youth' of today (body image insecurity, mental health problems, isolation, obesity, antisocial behaviour, an overdeveloped sense of entitlement, climate change anxiety, being perpetually offended), in many ways I wish it had been around when I was young.

As a just-shy-of-six-foot, awkward, opinionated, frizzy-haired, bisexual teen growing up in a multiracial family in the overwhelmingly Caucasian, conservative, image-obsessed environment of nineties Essex, I didn't feel I had that many role models at my immediate disposal.

There was my cousin (actually my nan's cousin – the generations in my family are messed up. Long story) who had the temerity to be single and happy well into her forties and who was into feminism, literature and leftie politics before they were cool, but she lived all the way in North London which meant, pre-email and with only a landline in the kitchen where everyone could overhear your conversations, I could only really communicate with her confidentially by letter.

There was my wonderful form tutor, Mrs Sheppard, who was young and acerbically witty, but teachers are restricted in how much they can tell you about their personal life, so it's not like I could ask her if she'd ever snogged a woman and, if so, where one might go in order to achieve such a thing.

And then there was my mum, who I now recognize is very aspirational, but when you're a teenager, you'll do anything you can to avoid being like your parents – which in my case involved staunchly refusing to give any care or attention whatsoever to how I looked or how I dressed, so as to rebel against my glamorous, ex-model mother and inadvertently further embed my reputation as a bit of a weirdo.

Other than that, role models were restricted to what I could glean from the pages of *More!* magazine, a biweekly teen publication most famous for having a cartoon at the back depicting sex 'position of the fortnight'. Back then, the media was even worse on the diversity front than it is now. Young women in the public eye were consistently very white, very thin and wore a uniform of trousers so low they skimmed their pubes. Except they didn't have any pubes because it was the nineties, so I should say 'where their pubes should have been'.

Of course, I could have gone hunting for obscure fanzines or caught the train to London and wandered around hoping to bump into someone inspiring who might befriend me and take me to an LGBTQ+ performance poetry event or similar, but between GCSEs, drama rehearsals, piano lessons and an all-consuming crush on the one with the good eyebrows from 3T (a boyband consisting of three of Michael Jackson's nephews – they had, like, one hit), there didn't seem to be much time for that. So, I just carried on feeling a bit alien and isolated, wondering what was wrong with me and why I couldn't have washboard abs and an older boyfriend with a car like 'everyone' else.

If social media had been around, I could have found people who showed me how to be different in a way that was badass. And, rather than have my access to them filtered through the prism of a media agenda, or what the journalist interviewing them thought was important (always, for some reason, 'what's your favourite pudding?'), I could have had direct access to their output – a hotline to their innermost thoughts. Or, a sanitized-for-social-media version of them, anyway. I could, with the right combination of clicks and follows, have found a community of people who 'got' and inspired me. At least in principle.

That's what social media is meant to do – plug you into a group with whom you find kinship, motivation and encouragement. Unfortunately, if we allow the choices of who populates our online wallpaper to be dictated by those pesky algorithms, we'll end up simply following who the people we follow, follow. In most cases, that's the people in your school and whichever is your favourite Kardashian/Jenner.

Finding your online role models therefore requires strategy and effort. As a first step, try this exercise, which I call 'curating' your feed:

STEP 1

Log into your social media account. Rather than scrolling as you usually would (one eye on something else, not really paying attention other than to make casual, half-arsed observations about, e.g. someone's shoes), do so mindfully. Spend a few seconds focusing on each post and notice how what you see and hear makes you feel.

Note down any thoughts you have.

STEP 2

Unfollow, mute* or delete anyone posting content which makes you feel anxious, insecure or triggered.

A note on this: as we will see later, there is a difference between feeling/being 'triggered' and 'challenged'. You can disagree with someone's point of view, which might make your hackles rise, but if their motivation is on point and they're not posting anything which, for example, contravenes human rights or potentially puts people in danger, then it might be worth leaving them in your follows as a glimpse outside of your 'slipstream' (see chapter 1).

---

* Further note: people don't know they have been muted, which is why it is the single most genius function ever to be introduced to social media. If there is a particular person at your school or college who you know will create drama if you unfollow them, you can just mute them for an easy life. I also find it particularly satisfying to mute trolls. Some of them get a kick out of being blocked (in fact, some of them list who they have been blocked by in their bios, which is the hallmark of a person with literally no redeeming qualities). By muting, they can continue screaming into the abyss and I don't have to see their nonsense.

STEP 3

Look at your feed again. Does everyone look a certain way? Does everyone have the same opinions? Note down what you think your feed needs, e.g. 'a broader range of different body types', 'more inspirational content that makes me feel motivated', or 'some people whose political views don't match my own'.

A note on visual diversity: it's not just finding people who look a bit like you, or share some common characteristics, which is important when it comes to role models. Evidence shows our body image satisfaction is improved when we are exposed to a diverse range of different body types, both like and unlike our own. So, it's good practice to try to make sure you are following people of different shapes, sizes, skin colours, hair types, etc.

74

STEP 4

Find three people you think represent a 'good follow', because they plug the gaps you have identified in your feed Since social media works using algorithms, you will now find more people like the ones you've selected in your 'suggested follows'.

STEP 5

If you want, you can ask everyone in your class or friendship group to follow the steps and note down their suggested follows and why they like them. An average secondary school class contains thirty pupils, so if you pool your role models, there will be ninety for you to choose from in order to diversify your feed.

THE DANGER OF EXPECTING 'PERFECT' ROLE MODELS

Whilst you will undoubtedly find people to admire in the three billion internet users worldwide, none of them will be perfect. How do I know this? Well, because no person in the history of humankind has ever been without fault.

Before social media, it was easy to make our role models fit our notions of perfection, because we had relatively little knowledge of them: what we didn't know we could auto-fill with idealized, if unrealistic, perceptions. That's how people like Freddie Mercury and Elvis ended up as icons – everyone has their own version of them in their head, which just handily happens to match with their idea of the qualities an icon should have.

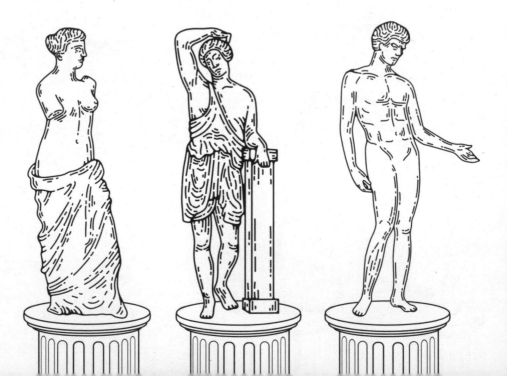

Now, we have no filter between the swirling randomness of our brains and our social media output, which means that occasionally we will mess up, or say or do something which displeases a proportion of the people who follow us.

There are two ways people tend to go with this. Either they abandon their role models as soon as they show any sign of disappointing imperfection, thus narrowing those they follow down to an ever-decreasing group of those who are probably highly problematic behind closed doors but have the good sense to only post rare and incredibly anodyne content. Or, they'll actually change their own moral compass so as to persuade themselves that the person they hero-worship **isn't** actually a terrible human and they were right to love them all along (see: fans of Donald Trump for multiple examples of this). Both of these reactions are, in my opinion, very much less than ideal.

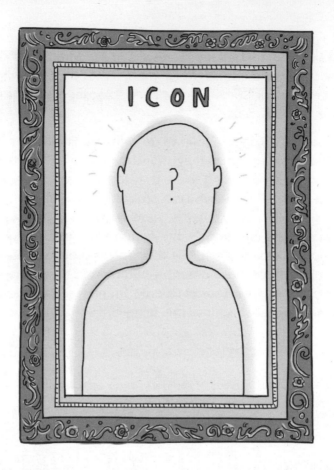

When selecting our role models, we should bear in mind that all people are complicated and all contain the propensity to be both amazing **and** total muppets. What attracts us to role models is not actually them in their entirety (after all, we often don't actually know the people we follow online) but aspects of their work, or character, which we respect/admire and wish to emulate ourselves. That remains the case, even if they tweet an ill-advised RIP message when a dictator dies, or receive sponsorship from a brand which just got busted for using slave labour. They probably didn't know and what you originally liked about them has not changed.

I'D GO SO FAR AS TO SAY IT'S IMPORTANT NOT TO HERO-WORSHIP

ANYONE.

YOU CAN APPRECIATE CERTAIN QUALITIES THEY HAVE AND ASPIRE TO CERTAIN ASPECTS OF THEIR LIFE, BUT IF YOU WHOLEHEARTEDLY BUY INTO ANY INDIVIDUAL AS YOUR OWN PERSONAL JESUS YOU'LL ONLY BE

DISAPPOINTED

ULTIMATELY.

Of course, that's not to say that you should give any person a free pass, or not call them out if you feel strongly. It's a question of whether they:

  a) acknowledge the problematic aspects of their behaviour and attempt to make amends;

  b) continue to repeat that behaviour; and/or

  c) have crossed one of your red lines.

Everyone's red lines are different and yours might morph over time to reflect your changing understanding of the world, but below are some of mine (to give you an idea of what I'm talking about):

• Sustained transphobia

Many social media users, particularly if they're over the age of forty, have only just found out that trans people exist. There's also a lot of misinformation out there about the issues, on some very mainstream platforms. I can therefore forgive a couple of misguided posts. If, after it has been been pointed out to them that they are being transphobic/spreading inaccurate information or anti-trans propaganda they double down and continue in wilful ignorance, I can't be doing with it. People who deny trans people their rights because it's a populist view and they know it actively damages a relatively tiny proportion of the population are BAD VIBES and I don't trust them.

• Antisemitism

Being as I am what might broadly be described as a 'leftie', there aren't many racists in my social media slipstream. However, I do occasionally stumble across antisemitism (hatred of Jewish people). Antisemitism is a sneaky sort of racism, because it leads to the idea that Jews aren't oppressed in the same way, say, Black people are. This is often referred to as being a 'model minority' and it also applies to people of Asian heritage – if, as a group, your educational and financial outcomes are better than the national average, this often leads to the perception that you cannot be a victim of racism and therefore people can say what they want about you.

There are a veritable metric ton of conspiracy theories on the web which centre around the idea that Jewish people are secretly controlling the world and therefore anyone who sees themselves as oppressed shares them as a common enemy. You know who also believed that? Hitler. If you're agreeing with Hitler, I'm going to go out on a limb and say your views won't lead to anything good.

• General annoyingness

When we are annoyed, we produce a chemical called 'cortisol', which is sometimes referred to as the 'stress hormone'. An imbalance of cortisol not only negatively impacts our mental health (it makes us more vulnerable to conditions like clinical depression and anxiety disorders, as well as interfering with our ability to focus, concentrate and make decisions), it can also affect our physical health by lowering immunity.

Whilst becoming annoyed is an inevitable consequence of living life, and sometimes very necessary in order to get stuff done, it's shrewd to try to minimize the amount of unnecessary annoyance we encounter, day to day.

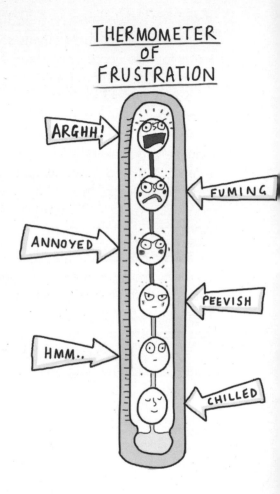

THERMOMETER OF FRUSTRATION

ARGHH!

FUMING

ANNOYED

PEEVISH

HMM..

CHILLED

I therefore make it my priority to unfollow anyone who does the following (IMO) incredibly annoying things on social media:

- **Posts trite inspirational quotes** such as 'if your dreams don't scare you, they are too small'. Eurgh. Jog on with that nonsense, please.

- **Slags off people who post selfies whilst posting a selfie,** e.g. 'I don't usually post pictures of my own face because people who do that are really vacuous and vain but today I have a special excuse for doing so because it's my birthday/book launch day/a Tuesday/My Face Awareness Day'. JUST OWN THE FACT THAT YOU THINK YOU LOOK NICE, FFS.

- **Faux-modesty/Humble bragging.** You know the type.

It's incumbent upon us all, I think, to work out what our red lines and irrational annoyances are, so we can allow for diversity of opinion in our feeds without spontaneously combusting through sheer frustration at the anger-making stupidity of our fellow humans.

HOW TO PICK PEOPLE YOU DISAGREE WITH

Being online means being part of a gigantic, global conversation which encompasses topics as disparate in their scope and importance as how we can solve the urgent issue of climate change to who is the prettiest cat in the world (The answer is mine. My cat. There. Done). Making progress involves seeing potential chinks in the armour of your own argument, as well as considering the perspective of others, and you can only do that by exposing yourself to perspectives which don't entirely match your own.

When looking for people whose political or social opinions are different from yours, but who won't make you feel anxious or triggered, here's a few questions to ask yourself:

• Does it seem likely that they actually believe what they are saying?

There are many people out there who have made a good living out of whipping up outrage storms on social media by deliberately saying terrible things. It's unclear whether they truly believe them, but they do often legitimize racist, homophobic and misogynistic viewpoints, so they're best ignored, lest we accidentally amplify their views.

• Is there solid evidence for what they are saying?

As explored in the previous chapter, you can find a study which literally 'proves' anything if you look hard enough. But if they are posting data from reputable sources, that's a good indication there is substance to what they are saying.

• Are their motivations good?

What do you think they are trying to achieve by posting what they do? Are they pointlessly playing devil's advocate because they have no skin in the game and nothing better to do that day, or does it seem like a genuine and thoughtful attempt to try to portray an alternative viewpoint?

• Are they open to discussion?

Are they engaging thoughtfully with people who are challenging and criticizing them, or are they just blocking them/replying 'HAHA, you're an idiot and I win'?

If the answer to all of the above is 'yes' and they don't cross any of your red lines, they're worth a follow.

SUGGESTED FOLLOWS

I'm not here to tell you who your role models should be. However, if you're looking for some ideas of the kinds of people who are out there, being marvellous, on social media, some of my suggestions are below. As you'd expect, many of them post content related to mental health and/or body image:

1.   Jamie Windust – @Jamie_Windust

Jamie is an award-winning non-binary writer, public speaker and model from London. They have written for *The Independent*, *Gay Times*, British *GQ* and *Cosmopolitan*, as well as authoring the book *In Their Shoes*. They were named as one of London's most influential people, in the storytelling category, by the *Evening Standard*.

If you're looking for someone who'll show you how to use fashion and make-up to truly express your individuality, whilst speaking eloquently on the issues affecting the trans community, Jamie's your one.

2.   Dan Richards – @TheOneArmedWonder

Dan was working for the army in Afghanistan when he was involved in a near-fatal motorbike crash in 2012. He lost his left arm and shoulder. Since recovering, Dan has run marathons, trained as a scuba instructor and pilot and done modelling to advocate for, and improve visibility of, people with disabilities.

3. Alex Holmes – @byalexholmes

Alex is a writer and podcaster who specifically focuses on men's mental health. He is a certified holistic health coach and trainee psychotherapist who seeks to support people with their emotional education. He hosts a podcast called *Time To Talk*, on which he speaks to experts in their field and is the author of *Time To Talk: How Men Think About Love, Belonging and Connection*.

4. Megan Jayne Crabbe – @MeganJayneCrabbe

Megan has been leading the body positive revolution here in the UK. Whilst in recovery from an eating disorder, Megan began a blog and Instagram account in which she celebrated the parts of her body which would have been airbrushed out of existence in other media – rolls, cellulite, belly fat – she sought to find the beauty in them. She now has more than a million followers and uses her platform to celebrate marginalized bodies. Just by following Megan you'll be exposed to a hella diversity.

5. Ellen Jones – @ellen__jones

Ellen is an award-winning campaigner who speaks and writes on LGBTQ+ rights, mental health, autism and gender.

In 2018, Ellen won the first-ever MTV EMA Generation Change award in recognition of her campaigning. In 2017, she was named Stonewall's Young Campaigner of The Year after running successful campaigns tackling LGBTQ+ inequality in schools and online.

6. Akala – @akalamusic

Kingslee James McLean Daley, better known by his stage name Akala, is a rapper, journalist, author, activist and poet from London. In 2006, he was voted the Best Hip Hop Act at the MOBO Awards and has been included on the annual Powerlist of the 100 most influential Black British people in the UK several times. He wrote *Natives: Race and Class in the Ruins of Empire* and is, in my opinion, the most thoughtful and intelligent person on the whole of the internet (and possibly in the world).

CHAPTER 4

HOW TO USE YOUR POWER AS A DIGITAL CONSUMER FOR GOOD

(INCLUDING HOW TO BE A GENUINE ALLY)

In this chapter, we're going to explore specific tips you can use to be an effective, responsible and positive digital consumer. Before that, though, I'd like you to consider the following three questions:

1.

WHAT DO I WANT TO GET OUT OF SOCIAL MEDIA?

2.

HOW DO I WANT THE PEOPLE WHO FOLLOW ME TO FEEL WHEN ACCESSING MY CONTENT?

3.

WHAT WOULD A STRANGER LOOKING AT MY FEED THINK?

How you use the tips that follow will depend, to an extent, on your answers to these questions so keep them in mind as you go through this chapter.

GAMING THE ALGORITHMS

We already know that social media harvests a lot of detailed information about us, using algorithms which share information across all the sites we interact with.

We also know that what we choose to engage with online is not a private decision, but something which is measured and fed back into the algorithm, which can then make more accurate and sophisticated guesses about our preferences.

So far, we've only considered the potential **negative** consequences of this. Yet, the fact that social media is designed in this way also gives its users an enormous amount of previously untapped consumer power, and that is **particularly** true if you are a young person.

Previously, before the advent of the internet/social media you only really had value as a consumer either after the age of fourteen, when you could legally have a part-time job and therefore disposable income, or tangentially via what your parents or other adults in your life might choose to buy for you. Now, you can tell the internet exactly what interests you and what you'd like to see more of in the future, because you are a consumer in the . . .

ATTENTION ECONOMY.

Companies and brands are, as a general rule, endlessly obsessed with what young people want and what they are interested in. If they can work that out, they can remain ahead of the curve, creating products and services which will appeal to the next generation of consumers. That means the online choices you make as a young person – what you click on, engage with and who you follow – hold **even more weight** than the average person. Your choices are indicative of trends which herald the future. You therefore have a stake in what that future will be.

IF YOU COULD WAVE A MAGIC WAND AND CHANGE SOMETHING ABOUT THE MEDIA, OR ADVERTISING, WHAT WOULD IT BE?

For example, you might like to change the way a certain group is portrayed, or see more businesses being transparent about their sustainability. Or you might just never see your hobbies and passions represented in mainstream entertainment.

By leveraging people, or brands, who are getting it right, you are ensuring not only their survival, but more content, services and products of this nature in the future.

As discussed in the previous chapter, there are three billion internet users worldwide, which gives you almost infinite choice as to where you spend your engagement and clicks.

HOW THE INTERNET CHANGED BEAUTY PARADIGMS

I know the power of these kinds of tactics because I have seen them play out in the arena of body positivity and visual diversity in advertising. As I've already mentioned, when I was a teenager, there was only one way girls could be considered attractive and that was to be very thin, very white and largely silent. Boys, conversely, had a choice of two blueprints – the athletic 'sports jock' type, or the arty and interesting muso type. There was never any acknowledgement of anyone who might not fit into those two gender binaries, or indeed anything other than this idea of a gender binary . . .

The beauty paradigm was dictated entirely by high fashion and media and who got to populate those industries was at the discretion of a very small group of powerful people who apparently had absolutely no interest in leveraging anyone who didn't look like Britney Spears or Freddie Prinze Jr. (Google him. He was in *EVERYTHING* for about three years in the late nineties).

But then, the internet changed all that. People who fell outside the traditional boundaries of conventional attractiveness started amassing enormous followings online. Fashion and beauty brands realized that if they didn't use these new 'influencers' to showcase their products they'd be missing out on a huge opportunity to access their fanbase. The previously elitist fashion club opened its doors to the likes of Ashley Graham, Tess Holliday and Winnie Harlow, none of whom would have made it by the narrow and prescriptive standards applied to their forebears. Now, the runways are graced by people like Paloma Elsesser, Anok Yai and Chun Jin and we have TV and movie stars like Amy Schumer, Lupita Nyong'o and Janelle Monáe because the public voted for diversity and the industry knew it had to adapt to survive.

IT WORKS.

AVOIDING CLICKBAIT

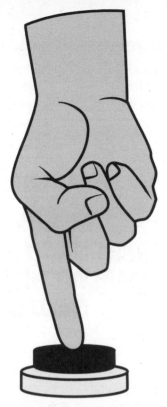

It also works the other way around. If you're drawn into content which you know logically isn't good for your well-being (or anyone else's) out of a morbid curiosity, you're still 'voting' for that piece of content with your clicks.

Professional outrage-mongers – whose entire careers depend on generating more and more outlandish and offensive opinions – rely on this type of interaction. By my reckoning, at least 80% of their clicks are people sharing their content alongside sentiments amounting to 'have you seen what this absolute gobfunnel is saying now?'. It doesn't matter. Algorithms don't know why you click on things (yet), just that you did. So, this type of content continues to be prominently platformed, spouting hateful rhetoric and keeping racism, sexism, homophobia and other deeply undesirable facets of society alive, because we (in part) enabled it.*

Literally about five minutes after I typed this, a friend of mine sent me a text message saying 'WHY HE IS SO VILE?' with a link to an article by an alt-right commentator slagging off a historical drama for casting a Black actor in the role of Anne Boleyn. I nearly clicked on it, just to see the extent to which he'd managed to get his knickers in a twist about it and his (no doubt) ridiculous reasons for doing so, then remembered what I'd advised you to do and thought better of it.

This is just one example. Think of it in the same way you might approach what you eat. Wholesome, nutritious fare will nourish your brain; junk will damage it. You know what content online leaves you feeling satisfied and enlightened and you know which looks tempting but ultimately leaves you feeling empty, angry or sad. Make a note of your answers to the questions below:

WHAT TRULY NOURISHES YOUR BRAIN?

WHAT IS YOUR ONLINE 'JUNK FOOD' (THE THINGS YOU FEEL COMPELLED TO INTERACT WITH BUT WHICH MAKE YOU FEEL A BIT SICK AND UNSATISFIED AFTERWARDS)?

Much like with healthy eating, you don't have to completely eschew online junk. We've all taken a sneak peak at something a professional troll has flung out into the cybersphere out of pure nosiness, for example. Just don't make it the bulk of your online sustenance.

EXPERT TAKE

'In terms of the dangers of clicking on clickbait, I suppose there's a scale. For the most part, it's harmless. In some examples, the only danger is that you get exposed to pop-up adverts and you generate revenue for a publication you might not want to generate revenue for.

'When it becomes dangerous is when clickbait is combined with fake news. There are a number of fake news websites out there that will essentially carbon-copy an existing reputable website's design and name, and then change the wording slightly. CBSNews.com.co is a good example. The website has now been taken down, but by using the Wayback Machine, you can see what the page looked like in 2016.'

James Perkins from Full Fact on the importance of avoiding clickbait

SHOWING SOME LOVE

Imagine there were only **100 people** on the whole of the internet. Now imagine all of them had happened to see a meme you'd made, because an influencer with a gajillion followers shared it on their Instagram. (Hey, this is a fantasy, no need to overthink the logistics).

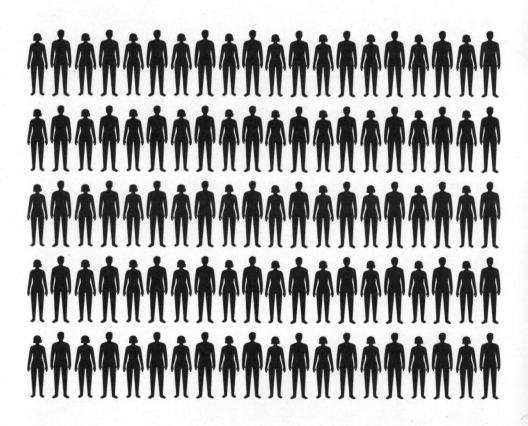

60 of the people who saw it will have no response whatsoever. To them, your meme is white noise, just something they notice idly whilst scrolling through their feed. They have no strong opinion of it one way or the other. Their brains barely register it.

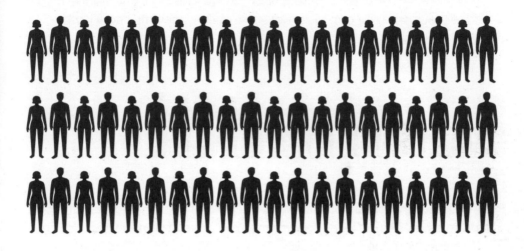

30 people see it, quite enjoy it, perhaps share it with their friends.

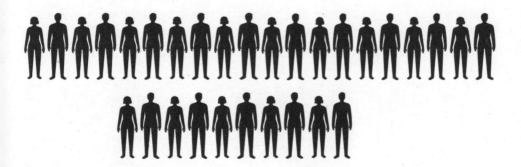

We're now left with **10** people who feel particularly strongly, for some reason. Some of them LOVE the meme because it speaks to them in a specific, emotion-inducing way. Some of them absolutely HATE it for the same reason. Of the latter, a couple of them are having a really hard time at the moment and they're looking for someone to take it out on. They don't just hate the meme, they also now hate YOU for making it.

The next day you log on to find you have **5** private messages. One of them says: 'OMG I *love* your meme! You are so talented and clever!' Two say: 'Your meme is rubbish.' Two say: 'YOU ARE EVERYTHING THAT IS WRONG WITH THE WORLD! I HATE YOU AND I HOPE YOU DIE.'

Which messages do you think will be the ones that stick with you, that you dwell on, that perhaps stop you from fully engaging with or enjoying the rest of your day? Which words do you think you will defer to when you're wondering how good you are as a content maker, or whether you are liked?

Psychologists have identified something called 'negativity bias'[14]. Our brains are hardwired to hold onto negative experiences more than positive ones. The evolutionary benefit of this is, I suppose, that we have more to learn from experiences that are painful, scary or anger-inducing than the times when we are happy and everything is fine. Back when we were tribespeople, it would have been advantageous for us to hold on to that time we accidentally walked into a cave containing an angry bear and escaped just before being chewed to death, to prevent us from making the same mistake again. Our brains are still pretty much the same as a caveperson's – we still have a propensity to cling on to anything which makes us feel uncomfortable, even if there is no benefit for us to do so. We also feel more driven to share our negative experiences than positive ones.

Numerous studies have shown we're more disposed to voice negative opinions than positive ones and we're also more likely to remember the criticism we receive than the praise. A by-product of what was once essential to human survival has led to a situation where the internet is not only full of pessimism and disapproval but also really doesn't reflect the way people actually feel in real life.

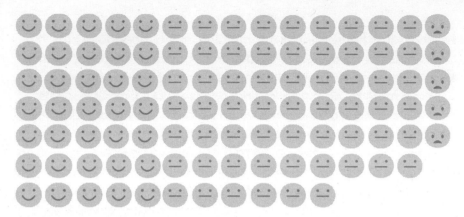

Remember, in my analogy above:

35% either liked or really liked your meme

60% were ambivalent

5% hated it

From the highly selective sample of the five responses you saw, you would think:

20% of people liked your meme

80% of people absolutely hated it, of which **50%** hated it so much that it caused them to hate you

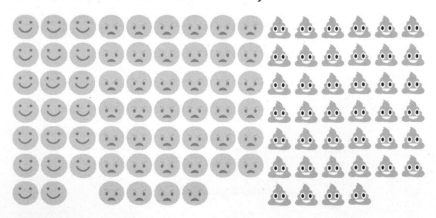

The great thing about being human, and what distinguishes us from other mammals, is that we can choose to override our basic instincts. Now we know 'negativity bias' exists, we can offset the consequences. In doing so, we not only make social media a more pleasant experience for others, we also ensure that the overall picture an objective onlooker would see looking at the commentary around a certain person, or piece of content, more accurately reflects what people really felt about it.

For example, you might:

• Say how much you enjoyed a book, TV show, meal or piece of content, tagging the creator if possible

• If you see someone is being targeted with a lot of abuse online, send them a direct message of support*

• If you really like another user's output, encourage your following to follow them too by giving them a shout-out

*Incidentally, as someone who is regularly on the receiving end of pile-ons, I cannot tell you how much these types of interventions mean. Everyone tells you to 'ignore the haters', but that's much easier to do if your inbox is full of people saying (in my case) things like 'your work has really helped me with my mental health' or 'I love your radio show' – it goes some way to offsetting the barrage of abuse which, no matter how many times it might happen, never stops being really quite unpleasant.

ALLYSHIP

Allyship is when one person lends their support, platform, time or energy to another person, or a cause which doesn't benefit them directly. They will do so for no immediate, obvious or tangible personal advantage. It often involves a person who has relative privilege showing allyship to someone who has relatively little privilege in pursuit of progress, or to give them a leg-up. Done right, allyship can change the world.

One of my favourite examples of allyship is Marilyn Monroe and Ella Fitzgerald. History will remember Ella Fitzgerald as one of the most talented jazz singers of all time. However, in the 1950s, despite her distinctive vocals winning her legions of fans throughout the United States, many venues were reluctant to put a Black woman on stage, regardless of how good she was.

Marilyn Monroe was friends with Ella Fitzgerald and a big fan of her music. Marilyn knew she had a huge amount of power, relatively, as one of Hollywood's most famous movie stars and decided to use it to help her friend out. She said to the owner of a famous LA nightclub called 'Mocambo' that if he put Ella on stage for a couple of weeks she would come and watch every night and sit in the front row with her celebrity friends. Knowing this would attract an enormous amount of free publicity, the manager agreed.

Fitzgerald's shows were a sensation, sold out every night, and Mocambo even added a week to her contract. Later, Ella told Ms. Magazine, 'After that, I never had to play a small jazz club again.'

Having said all that, allyship is context-dependent. So, whilst it might be true that white men are, on average, the most privileged group on earth, it's not true that every individual white man in the world is privileged. If white people are a minority in your school and have a hard time fitting in because of it, it might be more appropriate for the groups who would be described more broadly as 'minorities' to be the ones doing the allyship. It depends on who holds the balance of power in any particular situation, or environment.

WHY IS ALLYSHIP IMPORTANT?

There are obvious reasons why allyship is important: the world is unfair. It is divided into people who have too much and people who have too little and both groups have arrived there as a result of fairly arbitrary factors beyond their control, such as their year and country of birth, the colour of their skin, or how much money their family has. One of the ways we can bring about equality is by those who have too much sharing their privilege.

But if those types of arguments are a bit too hippy/pie-in-the-sky/let's-hold-hands-and-make-a-caring-circle for your tastes, think of it this way: Your future colleagues could be from literally anywhere in the world, or from any background. It will be important for you to be able to relate to and communicate with them.

ALLYSHIP IS A WAY
OF ACCESSING
DIFFERENT WORLDS.

IT INVOLVES PUTTING
YOUR EGO ASIDE
AND TRULY
EMPATHIZING WITH
ANOTHER HUMAN BEING
AND THAT IS, NOW
MORE THAN EVER,
A VALUABLE LIFE SKILL.

And if all that hasn't convinced you, think of the old adage 'you meet the same people going up as you do going down'. If you show allyship to someone, that doesn't mean they owe you a favour, but it'll probably make them more inclined to help you when it's your turn to need something.

'PERFORMATIVE ALLYSHIP'

There are tons of variations on the sentiment that when you do something for another human being or cause, it's only really a 'good deed' if no one knows that you did it, but I was first introduced to it via RE in Year 9 when we looked at Matthew 6:2 in the Bible:

'Thus, when you give to the needy, sound no trumpet before you, as the hypocrites do in the synagogues and in the streets, that they may be praised by others. Truly, I say to you, they have received their reward.'

If Matthew was writing for the internet era, he would probably say something like:

'Thus, when you want to support anti-racist causes, don't post a black square on your socials as hypocrites do on Instagram so that they can get likes. Truly, I say to you, this is performative allyship.'

Which is kind of true, to an extent. But then again you might also argue that by posting about a cause, you are drawing it to the attention of your following, 'raising awareness' if you will, and they in turn might be inspired to support said cause, thus ultimately benefitting it.

The difference between genuine allyship and performative allyship is often really subtle, for that reason. Take the black squares that people posted to their Instagram grids following the murder of George Floyd in 2020 in solidarity with Black Lives Matter.[15]. The point of that was supposed to be that you took that day to find and recommend resources which would benefit the cause. So you would tag in your black square, for example, a book on anti-racism which you were reading, or a grassroots charity paying the legal costs of people arrested and jailed at BLM marches, or an activist working in the area who was worth a follow. The black square was supposed to kick-start something: people doing the work to educate themselves and becoming involved in causes to further equality.

However, what ended up happening is people, businesses and brands just posted a black square with **#BLM** as if to say 'look at me/us and how nice and not racist I am/we are!' and then they just went back to posting selfies or photos of their dinner the next day and nothing much changed. That was performative activism.*

Is performative allyship and activism better than nothing? Perhaps. Social media reflects and, to an extent, sets the codes by which we live. If the people dictating the tone of the conversation are saying 'hey, it isn't cool to be racist/sexist/homophobic/transphobic' that's arguably a miniscule win, even if they don't really understand why they're saying it.

---

* Performative activism should not be confused with 'virtue signalling' or being 'woke'. Both of these are, in my experience, insults hurled by angry people trying to derail someone else attempting to show allyship and should be ignored. If someone accuses you of being 'woke' then keep doing you, boo, because you're probably doing something very important indeed.

THE FIRST RULE OF ALLYSHIP IS ACKNOWLEDGING YOUR PRIVILEGE.

I find dialogues around this on social media can be quite reductive and also have a tendency to conflate identity and privilege, which are not the same.

Let's take me as an example. I am of mixed ethnic heritage, I am a woman, I am from a working-class background, I am bisexual and I have a diagnosis of an ongoing mental health issue. On paper, it would be really easy to make every conversation about equality about . . .

ME, somehow.

But let's examine a little closer:

I am of mixed ethnic heritage. But I'm very light-skinned. Most people assume I'm white. So, whilst I am part of a multicoloured family and have been in the presence of a lot of racism in my life, I don't understand what it is to be directly on the receiving end of it. I have never had the experience of existing in Black or brown skin.

I am a woman. But I live in a country and a time where I have choices over my body and what happens to it. I have had access to an education, healthcare, I can vote, I can choose who I have a relationship with, I can choose whether or not I want to have children – that's **not** true of every woman in the world, even as I type.

I am from a working-class background. My parents are working-class, we didn't have a lot of money when I was growing up and I was the first in my family to go to university. **But** I did get a really good education, the chance to go to university and now I'm an author and broadcaster, which is, let's face it, a very middle-class job.

I am bisexual. But I am also married to a man. Being in a heterosexual dynamic means I have the option not to talk about my sexuality, if I choose, and that my partner and I will never be excluded or judged based on the gender mix in our relationship.

I have an ongoing mental health issue. This technically means I can describe myself as having a disability. **But** I am fortunate enough to have had access to a lot of therapy, which means I know how to manage it. I have supportive family and friends and exist in a social circle where there is literally no stigma whatsoever associated with discussing mental health. Because of my job, I have also had the privilege of interviewing, and therefore benefitted from the wisdom of, some of the world's leading experts in the field.

I'm really grateful, actually, because being me gives me empathy with a really broad range of people, but I don't suffer in the same way many of them do. That's a veritable ton of privilege, right there. So, it's clearly appropriate for me to try to use that privilege to help other people (something I endeavour to do every day).

While I'm on this, please DON'T text your Black/brown/gay/trans friend asking for advice on what to post to your socials in order to appropriately display allyship. Many Black people spoke about how their phones 'blew up' after George Floyd was murdered with white friends asking if they should get involved in online activism and what they should say, if so.

This is infuriating behaviour because:

a) It makes it look like you have just noticed that racism/homophobia/transphobia is a thing when they have been living with it (and probably talking about it) their whole lives.

b) You're asking your friend, in addition to living with the consequences of oppression, to teach you how to fight it and implying that if they don't, you won't bother, which puts them in an awkward position.

c) It's lazy. There's loads of information out there about how to do effective allyship – whole books as well as numerous articles have been written on the topic. If you care, you should take the time to do your own research.

THE **SECOND** RULE OF ALLYSHIP IS TO DO IT FOR ITS OWN SAKE, BECAUSE YOU GENUINELY BELIEVE IT'S THE RIGHT THING TO DO. NEVER EXPECT A 'THANK YOU'.

AND THE **THIRD**, AND POSSIBLY MOST IMPORTANT, RULE OF ALLYSHIP IS TO LISTEN WITH THE INTENTION OF UNDERSTANDING.

We are all entitled to an opinion, but we should take into account a person's lived experience when assessing how valid their take on a topic might be.

For example, if the topic was education in the UK, my opinion (as someone who visits an average of three schools a week) would be more valid than some random politician who last went into a school when they were a teenager and your opinion, as a young person who recently left (or is still at) school, would be more valid than mine.

If you told me something negative about your school experience, my job would be to try to find out how many other young people felt this way (i.e. how widespread the problem is), what potential solutions there might be and if I can help to bring those changes.

There's more information in the next chapter on how to campaign effectively, if that's something that interests you.

AND FINALLY . . . DON'T FEED THE TROLLS

The definition of a troll is a person who 'intentionally tries to instigate conflict, hostility, or arguments in an online social community'. They usually don't genuinely believe what they're posting.

Why would anyone do that? The answers vary. The most harmless types of trolls are just bored and get a kick out of provoking any kind of reaction. They're like that kid everyone knew at primary school who couldn't distinguish between positive and negative attention so used to deliberately stick Lego up their nose so they'd be sent to the school nurse.

But trolling also takes more sinister forms. A report by the Centre for Countering Digital Hate found some dangerous alt-right organizations were gaining traction and spreading misogyny and racism online by deliberately targeting liberal people with large followings. When the liberal commentator engaged with the troll, the troll's comment would be seen by the liberal's following. Whilst 99% of those followers would probably think 'that's awful', 1% might be intrigued and follow the troll. By doing this several times, the troll can broaden their audience.

The other type of dangerous trolls are the pundits, commentators and columnists who make a living from generating outrage. We all know the sort of people I'm referring to here – those who write or say deliberately provocative things with the specific intention of giving offence. As we know, media needs clicks in order to generate ad revenue and doesn't particularly care how it gets them. There are those who have carved out an entire career from expressing racist, sexist, xenophobic, homophobic and transphobic sentiments and watching gleefully as social media users inevitably lose their shiznay about it. It's a game played purely for reasons of wanting to gain money and fame, the unfortunate side effect being that they legitimize and normalize some truly awful ideas along the way.

The official guidance is, therefore, **never to engage with trolls**. It's difficult, however, and no one I know manages it 100% of the time. Trolls generally know exactly what to say to inspire the urge to clap back. They also adapt their language and tactics so they can fly under the radar of the 'community standards' of the platforms they operate on. If you can, mute, or block, and move on with your day. You might spend the next three days rehearsing clever comebacks whilst brushing your teeth in front of the bathroom mirror, but it's better than accidentally amplifying a toxic idea.

If you feel you really must respond to something troll-ish in nature, because you have a valid take or because it demonstrates a point you're trying to make, **always screenshot rather than sharing links**. That way, you're not directing your followers to the troll's profile/content.

EXPERT TAKE

'The online world and the offline world are not separate things. They are intermediated by the same things: people. We make social media. It's social, it's society, and society has the right to determine what the code of conduct is on that, as do the companies themselves. You can't align the freedom of speech argument with the right of these companies to make millions of dollars every year through advertising revenue. That gives them a duty of care to their users to ensure that their terms of service are fairly enforced.

'The reason why their terms of service aren't what the laws are on hate speech is because the laws around hate speech are really minimal. It's really difficult to be prosecuted for hate in the UK. In the US, it's impossible because of the First Amendment. So, the reason [social media] have terms of service is because that's what society and its users and its advertisers expect. And, of course, those are much more stringent.'

Imran Ahmed, chief executive of the Centre for Countering Digital Hate

POSITIVITY CHALLENGE

Most of us have been told 'if you can't say anything nice, don't say anything at all' at some stage in our lives. This is evolved into a general 'good vibes only' sentiment online. If you're anything like me, you'll find it really annoying. It implies we should all be walking around with rictus fake grins, air-kissing each other and making insincere comments like some kind of positivity cyborg.

Having said that, there's a happy medium between feeling like you can never be negative and putting a constant slew of bitching, ranting and general misery out into the world via your socials. This week-long positivity challenge, much like most medicines, is not meant for long-term use. It's something to jolt us out of our usual way of doing things and kick-start a habit change.

Note down your answers to the following:

What has inspired you in the past week?

Who do you know that's doing good in the world?

What was the last thing you heard or saw that made you feel like your country/city/area was a great place to live?

Who are your style icons?

What YouTube channel or TikTok feed would you go to if you wanted a guaranteed laugh or to feel better?

Which celebrities or public figures do you admire? Why?

For seven days, your challenge is this: each time you feel tempted to say something mean, or complain, or engage with a troll, instead take a deep breath and substitute with something relating to one of your answers above. At the end of the week, you can even tell your following that you have taken part in the Positivity Challenge, describe how it made you feel and tag five of your friends asking them to carry on the positivity into the next week.

	Bad thing I avoided and good thing I did
M	
T	
W	
T	
F	
Sa	
Su	

A NOTE ON TOXIC POSITIVITY

Positivity, like most things in life, is best enjoyed in moderation.

Whilst we should always aim to sprinkle our output with positivity, we shouldn't expect every response we get to validate us. Some people use the concept of 'positivity' to avoid accountability.

For example, a person might post something (unwittingly) which contains racist, sexist or homophobic content. They'll then receive several responses pointing this out to them. Rather than acknowledging their mistake and learning from it, they will hunker down and claim their social media is 'good vibes only' space. Or they will claim that all the criticism is 'bad for their mental health'. Whilst personal insults, trolling and abuse are forms of bullying which has a proven negative impact on mental health, being asked politely to reflect on the impact of your social media content is something different. We shouldn't confuse having good mental health with being happy all the time.

CHAPTER 5

ONLINE ACTIVISM

At the time of writing, 252 million people have used Change.org to create a petition since its inception[16]. And that's just one website. The internet is awash with other petition hosting-sites, containing squillions of calls for change, all competing for our attention.

Some, like Marcus Rashford's campaign to give children free school meals during the pandemic[17] or Amika George's to give all school-aged pupils in the UK access to free period products[18], successfully changed the world. Others are just as worthy and important but have barely seen the light of day.

So, if you want to use the internet to bring about change, how do you make your campaign stand out from the crowd?

So far, I have founded **two** successful, largely internet-based campaigns:

THE MENTAL HEALTH MEDIA CHARTER[(19)]

This a really simple set of seven rules for any person or organization who wants to speak or write about mental health in a way that is safe, responsible and doesn't perpetuate unhelpful stereotypes.

I created the charter in 2017, in partnership with the Samaritans, Beat (the eating disorder charity) and Mental Health First Aid England. Whilst all three of these organizations have their own (excellent) media guidelines, my aim was to boil it all down into something which was not only completely transparent, but which a busy journalist on a tight deadline could glance over just to check they haven't fallen into some of the most dangerous pitfalls when it comes to the way media portrays mental health issues.

To date, more than one hundred magazines, newspapers, radio stations, blogs, journalists, celebrities, businesses, schools and other organizations have signed up to the charter. We have an online community of about 5,000 people who share examples of good and bad media reporting on mental health and also help us to shape mini-campaigns by answering surveys and calls to action. We also have supporter badges people can buy online.

WHERE'S YOUR HEAD AT[20]

This campaign aims to change the way mental health issues are understood, and responded to, in workplaces. It does so in three main ways:

- **Education:** Going into workplaces and delivering education on mental health

- **Awareness:** Using celebrity ambassadors and media pieces to raise awareness of how mental health issues can affect people in the workplace and what we can do about it

- **Law change:** Ultimately, we want to change the law so that mental health first aid training becomes mandatory in all medium and large workplaces (in the same way physical or 'regular' first aid training is)

I co-founded this campaign in 2018 with Lucie Cave, who is chief content officer at Bauer Media and also the closest thing I've ever encountered to an actual, real-life superwoman. I won't lie, being in partnership with Lucie gave the campaign a massive head start. Bauer Media are the umbrella organization for lots of different media brands, including KISS FM, *Grazia*, *Heat* and *Empire* magazine. That reduced the usual amount of work associated with generating media interest/finding high-profile supporters hugely.

Having said that, awareness and support are only part of the job. Bringing about tangible, structural change is a lot trickier. Our change.org petition asking for the law to be changed has gained more than 200,000 signatures at the time of writing[21] and, aided by the then-Shadow Minister for Mental Health and all-round legend Luciana Berger, I delivered it to the Prime Minister in October 2018. Luciana then led a parliamentary debate in January 2019. A subsequent change of government, Brexit and COVID then derailed the entire thing and all of us were mightily annoyed.

Fortunately for us, in 2021 we were contacted by MP for Watford Dean Russell, who was elected on a manifesto promise to train 1,000 mental health first-aiders in his constituency and was due to put forward a motion in parliament, asking for the exact same law change we were calling for. Generously, he offered to team up and we adopted him as an ambassador for Where's Your Head At. He has done two speeches in Parliament which went down a storm and the bill is awaiting a second reading. This is the next stage in actually getting the law changed (the process is loooooooooong).

SO, FINGERS CROSSED . . .

Here's what I've learned from spending time at the helm of these two campaigns:

DON'T REINVENT THE WHEEL

If you've come up with an idea for a campaign, the chances are someone else has also thought of it, too. It's always a good idea to collaborate, where possible. If there is another petition or campaign out there which has similar aims, it's a better use of your time to throw your weight behind supporting that, than to try to create something from scratch. If you have personal experience of the issue you're trying to fix, the founder of the existing campaign will probably be really grateful if you get in touch offering to share your story and be an ambassador for them.

BE CLEAR ON WHAT YOU ARE ASKING FOR (AND MAKE IT AS SIMPLE AS POSSIBLE)

After dealing with all the crap involved in navigating life, people have, in my experience, a limited amount of excess brain space. Most people want to support good causes, but you have to be able to grab them quickly and paint them a really vivid picture of what it is you're trying to achieve. The simpler, the better.

HAVE AN 'ELEVATOR PITCH'

See where I described my two campaigns? Notice I summed each up in one or two sentences, initially, before giving you further details. This is really key, not just for getting support (see above) but also for any media coverage.

Try not to be vague. If your campaign is 'justice for . . .' a certain person or group of people, for example, tell us what justice looks like.

What are you actually calling for and from whom?

YOU CAN'T FIX IT ALL IN ONE GO

Don't aim to try to solve the entirety of a really complex social issue. Pick an aspect of it and really focus on that.

You will always have detractors who will try to make out that your

campaign doesn't go far enough. You're likely to have plenty of people getting in touch to explain why your proposed change won't benefit them, or that it won't eradicate inequality entirely. Make it clear that you're not trying to make the world perfect, just bring about one tiny step which will make things slightly better.*

The best way I've heard this described was by Writer and feminist Caitlin Moran on a podcast[23]. She said she imagined feminism like a patchwork quilt. We each have our square, and when you sew it all together you get a movement.

DO YOUR RESEARCH (HOW WIDESPREAD IS THIS ISSUE?)

In the first instance, I'd recommend asking your friends and family if they have ever experienced the issue you're trying to resolve, or if they know anyone who has. This will give you an indication of how widespread it is and also how it might look in different contexts.

Then, do your research – find statistics which can demonstrate how many people this impacts worldwide, in your country, or in your area. Then look for statistics which will illustrate the scope of the problem in a different way. For example, for Where's Your Head At, two statistics we use very often are:

1 IN 6 PEOPLE WILL EXPERIENCE A MENTAL HEALTH ISSUE IN UK WORKPLACES EACH YEAR.

THIS COSTS THE ECONOMY AN ESTIMATED £35 BILLION EACH YEAR[24].

If the statistics don't exist, you can gather your own. For example, at the Mental Health Media Charter, we created an online questionnaire which over 2,000 people completed from our online community (that's actually a pretty good sample size and is about the sample number most media organizations would look for to suggest your survey was robust enough for them to quote). The survey found 75% of respondents had seen irresponsible media reporting on mental health in the past year. We turned this into a moving video for our supporters to share.[25]

GRAB PEOPLE WITH A STORY

Whilst it's really important to anchor your campaign in solid statistics and evidence, that's not generally what intrigues people. To get the public interested in your campaign you need to draw them in with a really compelling story. It can be your own story, if you've had personal experience and you're willing to share it, or you can source case studies which demonstrate how the problem you're fighting really affects people, on the ground.

Make sure you have written consent from anyone whose story you use, especially if their experience isn't already in the public domain.

HAVE A CLEAR 'CALL TO ACTION'

What is it you want the general public to do? Do you want them to sign your petition, visit your website, share your video? Make sure you know this in advance and that every piece of content you put out related to the campaign contains this call to action, to maximize your growth.

BE PRAGMATIC . . .

How are you actually going to achieve this? Whose help do you ideally need? Who do you know already who might know someone who can help?

You also might have to work with some people whose values don't exactly match your own. That's okay – as long as you share a common goal and can mutually benefit one another.

. . . BUT DON'T COMPROMISE YOUR PRINCIPLES

That doesn't mean you have to sell your soul. Beware of anyone who won't acknowledge the role you played, is in it for the glory, or who expects your eternal loyalty and gratitude for helping you (see previous chapter on allyship).

GET AN EXPERT AND/OR A POLITICIAN IN YOUR CORNER

If your campaign involves law or policy change, it really helps to have either a lawyer in your ranks or a politician – preferably both. The law is antiquated, opaque and often dull-as. Understanding the nuances of how to actually bring about structural change – what are the right terms to use, the procedures involved, etc. – will be a colossal advantage.

It's worth emailing your local MP in the first instance. Make sure you include your address and (in theory) they then have to reply to you. Set out your elevator pitch and say you'd be hugely grateful for their

support bringing about this change. If you have no luck, I'd recommend researching local MPs who have previously spoken about the problem you're passionate about solving, rather than going to Secretaries of State (who tend to be uber-busy and get their minions to send you a standard letter full of gumf about how the government is dedicated to this issue and that's why they've committed to investing £2.7 million to something completely different but tangentially related over the next five years, blah, blah, SNORE).

MEDIA

It's okay if you don't know anyone in the media. Most people don't. I didn't when I first started campaigning.

Your local newspapers and radio stations are a valuable entry point into raising awareness of your campaign and building support. They tend to have their contact details clearly stated on their websites and you can ping them across your elevator pitch. The chances are they'll be interested in the activities of a local resident – particularly if they're a young person ('Teenager Engages in Philanthropic Activity Thus Thwarting the Selfish Stereotype' being a staple of local news coverage). Sometimes, national media pick up stories from local outlets and it's as simple as that. Sometimes, it takes a little longer to build the momentum necessary to get your campaign noticed nationally. Which brings me to . . . **Famous Ambassadors.**

Celebrity or high-profile support can help your campaign, but only if it happens in the right way.

Firstly, DO NOT contact a whole heap of famous people via your socials saying, 'hi please can you share my petition?' They will either ignore it or just impulsively share it on their feeds to make themselves look like good people, but without actually understanding what the campaign is about, or really caring if you're successful (see 'performative allyship' in the last chapter).

There are some high-profile people whose entire feeds are just other people's campaigns and no one bothers to click on them because they share one every five minutes. It's far better to have one influential person who really gets what you're trying to do and is able to explain it as and when an appropriate opportunity arises than to have fifty random celebs RTing your petition.

Really think about who you want representing your campaign. Any old famous person might sound impressive on paper, but bear in mind that, ultimately, anything they do or say could affect your chances of success, or your reputation.

A quick google will let you know whether someone has a history of making misogynist or racist remarks, for example, or if they have a history of peddling conspiracy theories (this could dent their credibility and, consequently, yours). You don't want to waste your precious time and energy defending a problematic person when you could be channelling it into your campaign. Tabloids love a 'this celebrity might *seem* lovely because they support good causes but actually . . . ' story so be prepared to see your campaign mentioned in this context.

CONSIDER YOUR APPROACH

You're much more likely to be successful if you identify a moderately famous person to help you raise awareness. Another campaigner, a YouTuber or a podcast host with a large following, for example, is much more likely to help you out than Beyoncé.

Being one such ever-so-slightly famous person, and having been on the receiving end of a ton of requests to help people with their campaigns, here are my tips, based on the ones I'm most likely to respond to:

- **Tell them you're a teenager.** Everyone's a sucker for a teenager trying to make a difference

- **Make it clear you know exactly who they are** and chuck them a compliment. Don't just send a generic email. Tell them you admired a specific piece of work they did. Flattery never hurts

- **Make it snappy.** Include a few details about your backstory, but keep it to a paragraph. People are busy

- **Be really clear about what you want from them.** There's nothing more annoying than an email which says 'I'm not sure what I'm asking you'. Wait until you do know. Do you want them to film a quick video explaining why they support your campaign, for example (takes two minutes and is much more effective than them just resharing your content, in my experience)

If you don't receive a response, try not to take it personally. It's almost definitely not a reflection on you, rather on your recipient's schedule/state of mind when you sent the message. Locate another potential ambassador and keep going.

NON-FAMOUS AMBASSADORS

Having said all that, you don't *NEED* celebrity ambassadors. 'Real' people* can be just as effective. If you have managed to find a group of people all directly affected by the issue you are trying to solve who are prepared to share their story across social media platforms that can be really powerful. Make sure your ambassadors know what your **call to action** is (see previous page) and to include it every time they speak about the campaign.

It's worth putting together a simple document for ambassadors with your elevator pitch, a couple of stats, any significant moments in the campaign so far and the call to action, so you're reassured that whenever they speak about it they're staying on-message.

---

* Because, as we all know, celebrities are holograms.

MERCH

Again, you don't *NEED* merch and it can be really expensive and time-consuming. If you choose to go down this route, however, you have three options (bearing in mind most campaigns are not-for-profit which means you can't just keep any extra money you might make).

1) Just charge people the cost per unit of the badge/sticker/whatever, plus postage (that's what I do with the Mental Health Media Charter badges. There's no profit. It's just about brand recognition/raising awareness);

2) Donate any profits to a charity working in the same area as your campaign; OR

3) Put any profits back into the campaign, e.g. buying more/different types of merch or using sponsored posts on socials to increase your reach.

If you don't have any money but you or someone you know has artistic flair, creating an eye-catching slogan which you can turn into a shareable meme is a good shout.

IF YOU HAVE AN ENEMY, AVOID 'AMPLIFYING' THEM

We've already touched on this, but it's worth stating again: if you're trying to make someone stop doing something, avoid drawing undue attention to whatever they're currently doing.

The campaign Stop Funding Hate (details at the back of the book) is a fantastic example of how to get this right. Its aim is to prevent the media from sharing messages which are inaccurate and promote hatred. They do so by 'making hate unprofitable', i.e. targeting the advertisers sponsoring media organizations.

For example, if a newspaper runs a piece which is both inaccurate and hateful, SFH will contact the companies whose advertising appeared in that issue of the paper saying 'do you really want your brand associated with this message?'. The newspaper then has to sit up and pay attention because, if that advertiser withdraws its patronage, they stand to lose a lot of money.

This is a much more effective strategy than simply sharing the offending piece, expressing disgust and tagging the newspaper (which, whilst it might generate a lot of outrage, ultimately just results in the piece being shared more widely).

SUSTAINABILITY (AND PATIENCE!)

Be under no illusions: successful campaigning involves a gigantic investment of your time and energy. It can also be really frustrating, wearisome and incredibly dull. You will have to say the same thing approximately 237,000 times before people get the message. You will suffer setbacks, you'll inevitably draw criticism from people who either think you're doing it wrong or who just don't like any sort of change. Reaching your goal can take years.

I'm not telling you this to put you off (the world needs more activists), rather to prepare you for the challenge ahead. Ask yourself honestly if you have the time to dedicate to this, right now? If not, can you assemble a team to share the workload? Is the change you're seeking something which will still be needed and relevant in five years' time?

Assume you're in it for the long haul.

GOOD LUCK!

CHAPTER 6

'TEACHING UP': HOW TO BRIDGE THE GENERATIONAL DIVIDE

I often ask teens about their relationship with the internet – one of the questions I'm asked most frequently is 'how can I make my parents understand that social media/phones/video games aren't all bad?'

It's an excellent question. As explored in the introduction, there's a difference in perspective between generations that can be really tricky to navigate, exacerbated by the fact that (in most cases) children know more than their parents about tech.

This throws off the traditional child/parent dynamic where they get to feel smugly wiser and more experienced than you and say things like 'I remember feeling that way when I was your age . . .'

If you're frustrated because your parents or another adult just aren't getting what you're telling them, try taking the following approaches:

• CONSIDER THEIR PERSPECTIVE AND THEIR MOTIVATIONS

Parents can seem really unreasonable sometimes, particularly when they won't explain *why* they have made a certain rule or think a certain way.

My parents had completely opposite discipline tactics when I was growing up – my **mum** always took the time to share her rationale and to detail why we weren't allowed to do something and what she feared could happen if we did. My **dad** was very much more of the 'because I said so' school of thought and believed it to be outrageously impertinent if we asked him to elaborate on any of his decisions. I found this endlessly frustrating at the time (many doors were slammed).

As an adult, I realized that most of the instances in which the 'because I said so' defence was invoked, it was because my dad didn't think he knew enough about what we were discussing. He was scared because it was something new or uncharted and he wanted to be safe rather than sorry, but without losing face by revealing his lack of understanding or knowledge.

If the person you're trying to win over is more like my mum:

Think of it as a gift: they're giving you an insight into their brain and letting you know they're open to compromise. Listen to what they are saying. Demonstrate that you have really taken time to consider their concerns and aren't just dismissing them as the baseless hysteria of the old and past it.

It's likely that the reasons given will have something to do with your health or safety. People tend to take extreme or inflexible stances on something when they are afraid. From your parent or guardian's point of view, one of the people they love and care about most wants to spend time in a place where they've been told, repeatedly and in no uncertain terms, that all the paedophiles, extremists, pranksters, cyber-bullies and self-esteem-bashers are lurking. And they're not completely wrong about that.

Let them know that you are aware of the dangers associated with using tech and are taking steps to safeguard yourself (there are tips in the 'staying safe online' chapter later in this book). Reassure them that, if at any point you are concerned about the motivation or identity of a person you are interacting with, you will talk to them about it. Maybe even give them this book to read, so you are both (quite literally) on the same page.

It might also be worth actually showing them the app or game in question – navigating them through it and demonstrating the different features so they can picture what you're doing when you're on there and know what you're talking about when you discuss it. Try to take a deep breath and be patient with them when they inevitably ask questions such as 'so . . . what . . . actually . . . is the point of all this?'. Chances are, they're genuinely curious as to what you're getting out of it.

If the person you're trying to win over is like my dad:

Bear in mind that this is about their identity, as well as their fears. When we're children, we look at our parents like they are gods in human form. We assume they are the fount of all knowledge and capable of solving any problem. And because we're young, don't know much and have quite basic needs, this is largely true. Our relationship with our parents is built, in the early stages, on them being able to provide everything we require.

Then we grow up a bit and start to realize our parents are fallible, just like everyone else. We also develop 'critical faculty', which is the ability to analyze information in context and figure out that our chemistry teacher probably knows more about a chemistry-related topic than our parents (unless said parents are chemists, of course). We start to look for wisdom from a variety of different sources and stop deferring to our parents on everything.

During our teens, we also experience neurological changes which make us resent our parents and think everything they do is a bit stupid and one of the reasons is that we experience a massive spike in a chemical called dopamine. There's good evolutionary reasons for this – we're establishing independence – but from your parents' point of view it's got to be hard to go from being your child's own

142

personal guru to being the source of all their irritation and sarcasm.

You'll get a much better reaction from your parent if you stroke their ego a bit. Avoid saying things like '[other parent/my teacher] said it was okay!' or 'all my friends are doing it'. That won't wash.

Try something like 'I really respect your point of view on this, so maybe together we could come up with a rule around screen time/ what age I'm allowed on apps that we're both happy with. Shall we both go away and do some research and then compare notes?'

• TAKE TIME TO EVALUATE HOW YOU'RE FEELING AND BE HONEST ABOUT THAT

A chat is two different world views, sets of priorities and moods colliding and the more you can know about the baggage each person is bringing in beforehand, the better it is likely to go. That includes taking time to introspect a little bit, work out how you're feeling and why.

It also helps with the sucking-up aspect of the conversation: I don't know anyone who wouldn't respond well to 'I'm feeling a bit angry/confused and I'm wondering if you can help me work through it'. It's acknowledging your flaws and vulnerabilities and appealing to their (and indeed most people's) innate need to feel useful and relevant.

• BE SMART WHEN PICKING YOUR TIME AND PLACE

If you're itching to talk to your folks about getting a phone/setting up a TikTok account/rules around video game times, don't just ambush them the next time you see them. People don't tend to give thoughtful or positive responses when they're stressed and busy, so if you jump out from behind a cupboard while your mum's in the middle of a work call or your dad's just had his face projectile-weed on whilst changing your baby brother's nappy, chances are you're not going to get what you want out of the ensuing conversation.

There's lots of evidence to show we have our best, most productive dialogues when engaged in joint activity, for example, whilst on a walk or drive. That's because the activity papers over any awkward silences, giving both parties time to think about what they want to say rather than just jumping in with their first reaction. It's also because when we're side-by-side there's intimacy, but without the intensity of eye contact.

Try to create conditions where a good conversation can flourish. Offer to go with them when they next go to the supermarket, if it's a drive away. Invite them for a walk around the local park. Offer to make them a cup of tea and sit side-by-side while you drink it. All of these things are going to win you pre-emptive brownie points and put your parent in a favourable, relaxed and receptive mood.

• WORK OUT WHAT YOU WANT IN ADVANCE AND WHY

What outcome do you want from this conversation? Is it for your parent to understand why the form of tech you're discussing is so important to you? Then you need to work out your own answer to that question before you tell them.

For example, you could argue that making content is a creative outlet for you – a way for you to engage in a hobby that in turn allows you to let off steam or develop a skill.

When it comes to the 'it's sociable' argument, you have to be careful. 'It lets me talk to my friends at school' is dangerously close to 'all my friends are doing it' and will probably be met with the classic 'if all your friends jumped off a cliff would you too?' response. Equally, if you say it's allowing you to converse with people outside of your usual social bubble, you might provoke the paedophile/extremists concern.

Again, it's worth showing your parent the site itself and the type of people and content you'd be engaging with. Revisit the 'role models' section of this book and work out what it is you're actually getting from the people you follow, so you can explain it clearly.

Work out your ideal scenario – for example, how long would your parents let you spend on socials/gaming each day, in a perfect world? Then . . .

. . . BE PREPARED TO COMPROMISE.

Your parents will probably have differing views on what constitutes reasonable access to tech. It's unlikely you'll get your dream scenario, but think of it as a win compared to where you were before you had the chat.

• BE PATIENT AND DON'T USE JARGON

When you're immersed in something, it's really easy to forget that not everyone knows as much as you do.

Imagine if you had a teacher who used only words you'd never heard before and if you dared to raise your hand and ask what they meant they sighed elaborately and said, 'Duh, it's so OBVIOUS. You are so stupid.' The likelihood is you aren't going to get the most out of that lesson. Similarly, if I ask a question in a talk I'm giving and no one raises their hand, I don't think 'wow, this audience is thick', I think 'I need to make more of an effort to phrase this in a way that's going to resonate with them'.

So, if your parent is a bit slow on the uptake, or asks a really basic question, try to take that attitude: it's not that they're being deliberately obtuse, it's just that this is new to them.

Think back to before you had a working knowledge of this particular piece of tech and of all the words and concepts you would have been unaware of. Now imagine you were explaining it to your past self.

Lots of people are 'kinaesthetic' learners – which means they can't properly absorb a concept if you just explain it to them or show them, they have to actually do it themselves before it 'clicks'. So consider letting your parent have a play around with your game/app (set them up as another user if this will interfere with your game play/reputation). If they enjoy it, they'll instinctually understand better why you enjoy it.

• KEEP THE DOOR TO THIS TYPE OF COMMUNICATION AJAR AT ALL TIMES

If possible, it's better not to talk to your parents only when you want something or if there's a problem.

If you get into the habit of chatting a little every day, this will build the trust necessary for them to believe they can give you a certain amount of freedom and you won't immediately become a totally addicted, monosyllabic tech-zombie/join a Neo-Nazi organization/bombard all the girls in your school with unsolicited pics/give all the family's money away.

You don't have to talk about tech every day, it's a question of keeping the door of communication ajar so that if you ever need to step through it, for example if you want to honour your promise of talking to your parents about any concerns you have about other social media users, you can.

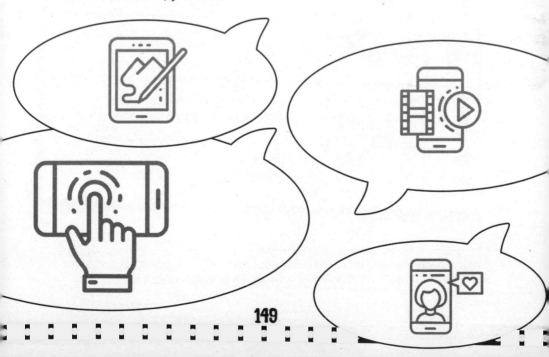

Lots of families I work with tell me they use the 'rate your mood' chat for this: every day when you get home from school/college, or they get in from work, or maybe over dinner, you and your parents/siblings rate your day from 1–7*, 1 being 'I dropped my laptop down a drain and then a rabid dog bit my arse as I was trying to retrieve it' and 7 being 'the sun was shining, birds were singing and I skipped around all day smiling to myself'. You can then ask 'what's happened to bring the number up or down from yesterday?' and 'what would need to happen to make the number higher tomorrow?'

It's a nice, fairly quick little ritual that keeps you all connected.

---

* When people are asked to rate LITERALLY ANYTHING from 1–10, they always say '7' without really thinking about it so that's why the scale is 1–7.

• ASK THEM TO PRACTISE WHAT THEY PREACH

Have they said 'no phones at the dinner table'? That should include them. Is the rule 'no internet after 8 p.m.'? Ideally, the family router should go off at that time to stop anyone going online.

The rules we create around tech use are theoretically to ensure we maintain healthy boundaries, curb the more addictive aspects and are able to function in other areas of our lives, and they're just as relevant to adults as they are to children and teens. Creating rules as a family brings you closer, squashes any lingering sense of unfairness and removes the notion that anyone is being specifically targeted or punished.

• ASK THEM TO TRUST YOU AND SHOW YOU ARE WORTHY OF THAT TRUST

If your parent is popping their head into your bedroom every five minutes to check you really are doing your homework rather than playing *Fortnite*/doing TikTok dances, that's going to build resentment and prevent you both from actually doing what you need to do.

If you have made an agreement with your friends that none of you will be on socials between certain, pre-agreed hours to allow you to focus on your studies, make sure your parents are aware of that. Explain that if they see you on a laptop or tablet between those hours, it's because you need it for your homework or revision.

Again, honesty about how it makes you feel when they're constantly checking up on you might help here. Say something like 'when you do that, it makes me feel like you don't have faith in my abilities or are accusing me of lying and then I get upset, which interferes with my ability to study' rather than giving into the temptation to shout **'FOR. GOD'S. SAKE. MUM. GO. AWAY'**.

A lot of the parents I talk to feel like their children are part of a 'guinea pig generation'. They believe (with good reason) that we won't truly understand the impact technology has on brain development, behaviour and mental health for another twenty years, when governments around the world will then be forced to issue more definite public guidelines around safe use (a bit like they do with alcohol, now).

Until such time, they're feeling in the dark, trying to apply their best judgement to something they're learning about at the same time as, or sometimes after, their kids. You can understand why this makes them jittery and why they sometimes get it wrong.

As we know, when it comes to anything that's addictive, the evidence shows there are two groups of young people most at risk and they're at either end of the spectrum: those whose parents take a zero-tolerance approach and say they're not allowed a phone until they're eighteen are just as at risk of developing unhealthy habits around tech as those who have absolutely no rules around its use and whose parents just give them a phone and say 'do what you like' in Year 6. What we're looking for is a happy medium and that's something which has to be arrived at through dialogue, compromise and everyone knowing as much as possible to enable them to make informed choices.

Think of it in those terms: the more knowledge your parents have, the better they'll be able to have the discussion in a rational way and you, as someone who has grown up alongside the internet, are in a good position to educate them.

CHAPTER 7

THE YOU WHO LIVES ONLINE

WHO IS THE YOU WHO LIVES ONLINE?

However noble our intentions, it's really difficult to give a genuinely, three-dimensional, accurate impression of who we truly are on social media. Online content is always missing some sort of crucial context which would help others to make sense of us.

Pondering the relationship between our online and 'real' selves reminded me of a lecture I went to by a music journalist called Paul Morley about icon David Bowie. Anyone familiar with Bowie will know he created several alter egos throughout his career, most famously an alien rock star called Ziggy Stardust. What most people don't know is that, according to Paul Morley and several other commentators who have studied Bowie's career, he shaped his personas (at least in part) in response to the feedback he got from his audiences. So, in many ways, Bowie's fans were part of his continual evolution because they held up a mirror to his previous incarnations.

Being on social media is very much like that. We create content with our following in mind, seeing ourselves reflected back through their gaze, changing our online behaviours according to their responses, anticipating what they might like and engage with. We therefore shape a character based on our understanding of their expectations. Also, like Bowie, we borrow bits of our peers' personas that we like, emulating their behaviour and ways of expressing themselves (Ziggy Stardust was reportedly an amalgamation of singer Vince Taylor, a sixties psychobilly performer called The Legendary Stardust Cowboy and the fashions of Japanese Designer Kansai Yamamoto). The difference between us and Bowie (other than that most of us aren't visionary geniuses making seminal art which will change the world) is that his alter egos weren't as directly interchangeable with his true self. He always knew they were parts he was playing. His name wasn't even really David Bowie, it was David Jones.

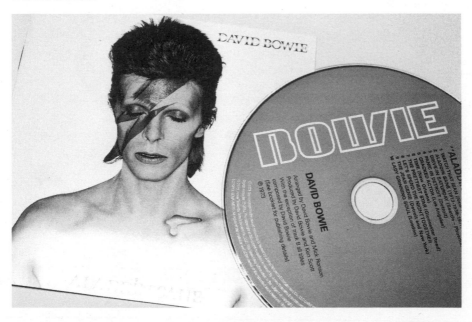

The issue with our online alter egos is that they're an unrealistic, and exaggerated version of us. When we post about ourselves, it's most often who we wished we were, rather than who we genuinely are. The reality of living inside our own heads will never quite match up.

It's strange, then, that when the You Who Lives Online (**YWLO**) is criticized, more often than not our response is to internalize that negativity as a reflection of our true selves. It's the worst of all worlds – when we're praised on social media, we dismiss it because we know, deep down, that it's not an assessment of our true selves ('they wouldn't say that if they really knew me'), but when the analysis of YWLO is negative, we take it to heart. As we have already explored, the superficial validation we get online is also very addictive, so we carry on chasing likes even though they rarely hit the spot and give us the recognition we crave.

Similarly, we have a responsibility to ensure the YWLO is representing us in a way we are proud of, because their actions can have a very real impact on the people behind the other YWLOs they interact with. YWLO is our ambassador out in the World Wide Web and their actions reflect directly upon us, even if they don't exactly marry with our original intentions.

The best way I've found to visualize it is this: if you've ever read or watched *His Dark Materials*, your YWLO is your 'daemon'*. It is separate from you and yet it is always close by and your experiences are inextricably linked. When something happens to our YWLO, we feel it just as acutely.

---

* His Dark Materials *is a fantasy trilogy written by Philip Pullman, which was made into a (brilliant) BBC TV series beginning in 2019. In Pullman's world, every person has a 'daemon', which takes the form of an animal. The animal is representative of the kind of person they are daemon to (shady characters in the series often have snakes or spiders for daemons, whereas heroes have things like noble wolfs and perceptive hawks). Whilst the animal behaves independently of their human, they are a sort of physical manifestation of their soul. A human and their daemon can't be physically separated and if a daemon is hurt or killed, the same thing happens to their human and vice versa. See? Very much like YWLO.*

'THE SPACE BETWEEN'

Even though our online self will never give a completely accurate understanding of who we are to the casual observer, it is important that the parts of ourselves we do reveal on social media are as authentic as possible. That doesn't mean we should feel obliged to 'overshare' if we're not comfortable doing so, more that we should always strive to be as accurate as we can in each moment.

We have already explored the notion of 'the space between' who we are and the person we present to the world. According to psychologists, the further the distance between these two people, the lower our self-esteem will be and the greater the chances mental health issues will arise.

Look at your feeds and ask yourself the following:

• **What impression am I trying to give and why?**

• **Is the person I'm looking at recognizable as the person I consider myself to be?**

• **Did I post this because I had something to say or because I was seeking validation/attention?**

• **If only my close friends and family, who know me and have my best interests at heart, could see my social media, would I have posted the exact same content?**

• **If someone only knew me from socials and then met me IRL, would they be shocked at the contrast between the impression I give online and who I am the rest of the time?**

The last question is a particularly pertinent one. In 2021, journalist Laura Andrades wrote a piece for *The Guardian* exploring some teenagers' apprehensions about meeting people they'd met on social media IRL. The piece explained that many young people feel nervous revealing their real, flawed selves after being introduced to a potential love interest via filtered and Photoshopped selfies and carefully selected soundbites.

Inherent in this worry is the idea that our online selves are somehow better, because we consider some aspects of ourselves shameful. But we should remember that our YWLO is an avatar, a cartoon, a person it isn't possible to be 100% of the time and that applies to everyone. We should see socials as an opportunity to understand the gist of someone, to draw some broad outlines. Meeting that person in the flesh is a chance to colour in the spaces in between.

LOOKING AFTER YWLO - BODY IMAGE

Supermodel Cindy Crawford once famously said,

'I WISH I LOOKED LIKE CINDY CRAWFORD.'

Every photograph of her had been the result of the input of a dedicated hair, make-up and style team, expert lighting and Photoshop so that her image bore little resemblance to who she really was. She was hinting, I suppose, that she thought she might be a 'disappointment' IRL. In the age of internet, we are all Cindy Crawford. And not in a good way.

Yet, there are so many aspects of the impression a person gives, and therefore how appealing or attractive we find them, which can't be captured in a photograph.

Think of the person you like best in the world. Chances are, you're thinking of the way they laugh, or something they say a lot, or how you feel when you are around them, rather than how they looked in the last selfie they posted.

Now think of someone you know IRL and fancy. Again, it'll be as much about how they move, smell and sound as it is what they look like.

In my twenties, I was something of a professional internet dater (I went on about three dates per week just for shiggles and wrote about my exploits for a London lifestyle magazine and then later for a newspaper). I learned never to base my expectations of what a person would look like from the photos they posted to their profile. On a very basic level, it wouldn't matter how many pics I'd seen of my date, I'd still always have difficulty picking them out of the crowd wherever we'd agreed to meet. When you know someone, you recognize them by their gait and their body language as much as their static physical features. By the same token, my dates were often surprised at how tall I am (even though I'd listed my height in my profile). This is because we tend to think of tall people as being thin and looking slightly 'stretched'. I'm a curvy tall person and therefore don't look tall in a photo unless I'm standing next to an average-sized person or measurable object for scale.

Really, you have to be in someone's presence to know if you really click. No doubt, dating gurus would say it's all to do with the pheromones we secrete, and they're probably right, but it's also to do with things like how their face moves when they talk and whether their eyes light up when they get enthusiastic about something.

Two YWLOs can establish a tentative connection, but it's no guarantee their real selves will hit it off. Similarly, people we might swipe left for on Tinder could be our perfect match, or at least a person we could have a lot of fun with, if we met them in a different setting. Unfortunately, it seems we're spending an awful lot of time and energy trying to emulate our YWLOs, who exist not only in a world where their perceived 'flaws' have often been filtered and airbrushed out of existence, but also inhabit a space where their insecurities are seized upon and magnified for profit.

Having said that, body image insecurity is very much *not* an invention of the internet. People have felt anxiety about the way they look since the first Homo sapiens glanced into a puddle and realized the reflection they saw was them. Probably.

However, social media has definitely changed the way we relate to our physical selves. It has also, I believe, created more equality in the way people of all genders experience negative feelings around how they look – and not in the progressive way you might hope.

Traditionally, women and girls have existed in a culture in which they were taught that how they looked was more important than who they were. But now, boys and men also inhabit an online world in which they're told, ruthlessly and relentlessly, that they don't measure up, that they are flawed and need fixing. This might go some way to explaining why eating disorders in men rose by 70% between 2010 and 2016, according to the Royal College of Psychiatrists.

EXPERT TAKE

'It's not surprising that we see body image issues arising when young people – particularly girls – become social. When they're aware of others, when they're further aware of their reflection in other's eyes and therefore they're more aware of themselves. So, that idea of looking in various mirrors and being reflected back is as old as time. It's how we construct identity. And usually what would happen is a person who has a vested interest in us – maybe a friend, a parent or a teacher – would say 'okay, you're trying to be this person . . . ' and they would kind of mould through that process.

'The difference these days is when they construct identities as kids they hold them up to people who don't know them, who don't have a vested interest in them becoming the best, or truest, or healthiest version of themselves. But, worse than that, they're holding them up in places that have a vested interest in making them feel insecure so they can sell them products and that becomes a big problem.'

Dr Linda Papadopoulos, psychologist

And yet, social media can also have a positive impact on how we perceive our own bodies and those of others. Trans and non-binary people, for example, whilst likely in a tiny minority in their schools, hometowns and communities, can find other bodies like theirs online and be inspired by the journeys of other people like them.

The internet also exposes us to greater diversity. By definition, there are far more people online than you could ever see with your human eyes during the course of a lifetime. Numerous scholars have concluded that the key to feeling good about your appearance is to surround yourself with as much diversity as possible in terms of the body types you are exposed to.

I have seen how this works, first-hand. In 2018 I was the presenting expert on a Channel 4 TV show called *Naked Beach*. The show was based on a piece of research by my co-presenter Dr Keon West. His study found that people who have low body image satisfaction can increase positivity around how they look by spending time around naked people of all shapes and sizes. We therefore sent

people whose lack of body confidence was stopping them from, for example, socializing, to live on a Greek island for one week with eight naked body positivity campaigners. We used Dr Keon's scientific scale to measure their body image satisfaction and self-esteem before and after the experiment.

I wasn't really surprised that all the participants felt much better about the way they looked when the week was up. In addition to representing a diverse range of bodies, the body positivity campaigners are some of the most inspiring and relentlessly cheerfully optimistic people I've ever met. It's pretty much impossible to feel low whilst around them. What was perhaps more surprising was that the effect lasted. The show aired in May 2019, almost a year after we filmed it, and the participants had managed to maintain their higher body image satisfaction and self-esteem during that time. This, I put down to social media.

The participants had followed the eight body positivity campaigners from the show on their socials, which, as we know, use algorithms to measure our preferences, so would have suggested more body-positive and diverse feeds. Every time they logged into their account in the year after the experiment ended, their online wallpaper would have been full of content which enhanced their well-being by emphasizing and reiterating the lessons they had learned whilst filming the show.

There is a lesson to be learned here. When we see diverse bodies online, it's usually in the context of knowing a little about the people who live inside those bodies. Naturally, we therefore respect those people more than anonymous models on billboards or in magazines. Social media therefore has potential positive power which traditional advertising does not.

When considering your online role models (see chapter 3), visual diversity should be a big part of your thinking.

YOUR SECOND REACTION

A psychology teacher once told me:

'YOUR FIRST REACTION TO SOMETHING IS ACTUALLY WHAT SOCIETY HAS INSTRUCTED YOU TO THINK. YOUR SECOND RESPONSE IS THE REAL YOU.'

So, if your first reaction on seeing a body type you're not used to is 'eurgh, that's disgusting! I don't want to look at that!' it's probably because you have been brainwashed into thinking that way by a culture which insists there's only a few, very narrow and specific ways, to look 'acceptable'. If you find yourself doing this, take a deep breath and think – **really** think – about the person who lives inside that body. Chances are, they're not so different from you. Imagine what it might be like to be them. Now look again and try to be kinder.

This won't happen overnight. But influencers have recently been making features, or celebrating aspects, of their human body which society tells them it would be more prudent to hide. **@stephyeboah** for example, puts golden highlighter on her stretch marks and talks about how beautiful the patterns they make are. **@harnaamkaur** has polycystic ovary syndrome and celebrates the facial hair she has as a result.

It really makes you think — who told us stretch marks and scars were shameful? Who made up those rules? Loads of people have them and it's just a pattern on skin. If the skin were a piece of marble, we would find that same pattern aesthetically pleasing.

It's this kind of questioning which can represent a way out of the prison of negative body image.

LOOKING AFTER YWLO - ONLINE SAFETY

It's safest to assume there is always someone trying to use the information you post online in order to scam you. This can happen in a variety of different ways — applying for loans using details about you they've gleaned from your output; hacking your socials, changing the passwords and then demanding money to give you back control; or getting your bank details when you type them into a website using a shared network are just a few examples of how hackers operate.

To avoid one of these nightmare scenarios, make sure you follow these basic safety tips:

1. Always use strong passwords.

Sounds obvious, but don't make your password something that a person could easily find out about you from your output on your socials, like the name of your pet, your middle name or your football team.

2. Use two-factor authentication.

This means you'll get an alert on your mobile phone and/or email if someone is trying to access your account. You can then verify whether or not it's really you.

3. Think carefully about how much personal information you're sharing publicly.

Those 'yaaaaay it's my eighteenth todaaaay' posts are actually telling anyone watching exactly what your date of birth is. If you or someone else happens to post a pic or video in front of your front door, that's your house number you're showing. If you're taking a photo of a surface, make sure there's no carelessly slung bank cards or envelopes with your address on in vision.

4. Only use secure websites, if possible.

The 's' in https stands for 'secure', so it's best to stick to websites with this in their URL. If you're going to input your card info, make sure you can see a little padlock sign in the browser (this means the website is protecting your information). Asking apps to store your card details might make it easier to purchase things but it also means if someone manages to hack your account they can go on an ordering spree at your expense. Consider entering them fresh each time. Where possible, use a third-party website like Paypal to make payments.

5. Don't click on phishing links.

You probably know about those emails you get, seemingly from someone in your contact list, that say things like 'OMG I didn't know this about you . . .' with a link to click (and not to do that). Be aware, people also send these types of phishing links via DMs. They can look really credible, too (recently an account that appeared to be verified, had hundreds of thousands of followers and was claiming to be a department at Instagram targeted users telling them their blue ticks would be taken away if they didn't fill out a form. The form involved typing in their password and those who didn't have two-factor authentication (see above) had their accounts seized. The hackers then demanded money to give them control of their accounts back).

6. Always log out.

Especially if you are using a shared network, make sure you log out of any website or app you're using.

LOOKING AFTER YWLO - DIGITAL SELF-CARE

Of course, keeping YWLO safe isn't just about protecting your personal information, it's also a question of taking care of your emotional safety and mental health.

I first became aware of the concept of 'digital self-care' via a remarkable woman called Seyi Akiwowo, who founded and runs the charity Glitch (you can find details of both at the back of this book). Seyi explained that she had to temporarily mute the hashtag **#BlackLivesMatter** following the murder of George Floyd in May

2020. As a Black woman, Seyi understandably found it traumatic to log into her socials every day and see pictures and videos depicting violence perpetrated towards people who looked like her and her family. It wasn't that she didn't support the call for racial equality (obviously), it was that she had been dealing with racism her entire life and she needed a bit of time to rest and calibrate her thoughts before deciding how best she could be useful during this time of renewed interest in the movement.

As well as making smart choices about who you follow and asking yourself what you want your social media experience to be, which we have already covered pretty comprehensively, digital self-care also involves feeling confident to say no to the things you don't want to see, or be part of.

Remember:

• You don't have to be on every app

• You don't have to comment on every trending topic

• If everyone is jumping on a campaign bandwagon, you don't have to partake. They've got this. Sit this one out if you feel tired, or triggered

• Apps now give you the option to mute certain hashtags or people from your feed, so if there is something that stirs up latent trauma, or you just find super-annoying, you don't have to see it

Taking control of your social media experience so it's nourishing, rather than battering, your brain requires constant vigilance. But it's definitely worth the effort. The difference between practising digital self-care and not is like the difference between having a faithful dog in your bedroom or an ill-tempered dragon who might fry you at any moment. The latter sounds exciting, but would quickly become incredibly stressful and exhausting.

EXPERT TAKE

'Digital self-care is a concept which allows you to have a flourishing online presence but not at the expense of your mental health.

'Be mindful about what you upload online – know where it can be taken. Not everyone you interact with in the online space has the best intention. Be critically engaged with who you follow and what you're taking and consuming. In addition to screen time, you also need to think about what you're digesting . . .

'The first step is to really think about where you want to be online. There's FOMO about having to be on every app and every platform . . . What gives you energy and what is sucking your energy? Have a social media audit. Part of that is looking at who you follow. Ask yourself "where am I in this season of life and what do I want to be seeing?" If you're starting sixth form, for example, you don't have to follow everyone you made friends with in Year 7. You signed their shirts to say goodbye when you left school – maybe that also requires you to say goodbye online as well.'

Seyi Akiwowo, CEO and founder of Glitch

WHAT TO DO IF YOU'RE PILED ON

At some point, many people find themselves at the centre of a social media pile-on. This is a symptom of the outrage culture we've already explored, but also of the fact that social media plays into some of our worst tribal instincts as human beings.

A pile-on happens when a user posts something which is considered outrageous, misguided or offensive and their content is shared and commented on by people wanting to express their disapproval. All it takes is for one high-profile account to join in and it can lead to you being the focus of their followers' attention.

This has happened to me approximately **four zillion times** and these are my tips for getting through it:

1 If you can (and it takes Herculean amounts of strength) log off for a couple of days. The pile-on will die down in 24–48 hours and you're in a much better position to assess what happened and why if you're not dealing with someone being mean about you every three seconds.

2 Ask yourself whether there is any validity in what is being said. Have you been misunderstood or have you posted something without thinking about who it might hurt? If the answer is 'yes' this gives you a chance to clarify and/or apologize.

3 If you choose to apologize, do it properly. Don't 'do a politician' and say 'I am sorry if people are offended but my remarks were taken out of context'. That's not an apology in any meaningful way. Just say 'I'm so sorry, I didn't think before posting this and on reflection it was a really stupid thing to post. I've deleted it now and sincerely apologize to anyone who was affected by my content.' Or something along those lines.

4 If there's no validity in the criticism being aimed at you, then try to DO NOTHING. Resist the urge to reply (if you reply, it means your followers will see the conversation and you run the risk of amplifying trolls). Rise above it, knowing you haven't done anything wrong. You can sleep at night and that's all that matters. You'll never be everyone's cup of tea.

5 There's some really nasty, organized groups of social media users out there who pile on women and minorities in an attempt to bully and harass them. If this happens to you, screenshot everything, then keep them in a file so you don't have to see them every time you look at your phone. Report it to the social media companies and, if you genuinely feel your safety is at risk (e.g. if posts include private or identifying information about a particular individual on the internet, with malicious intent, including death threats), tell the police.

EXPERT TAKE

'I genuinely think there is a sense of the world slipping away from certain people and of the world not making sense to them anymore. There is a standard of right and wrong that has emerged and they have somehow found themselves on the wrong side of it, in a way that they don't understand . . . It's a sense of feeling attacked, even if you're not being attacked.

'When they see things they believe have been "cancelled" or what causes Twitter storms, they feel they are being told they're on the wrong side of history. Often, the people who are expressing those ideas become a target and I genuinely think it's a fear reaction. It's scary to be told that the world might not have been as you have always seen it.'

Anonymous person who works at a social media company

CONCLUSION

'Life through a phone is a lie . . . like a diagram from physics lessons, the one on that Pink Floyd album cover – a beam of white light refracted in a prism, splintering and fanning out as a rainbow'

From Who's That Girl? *a novel by Mhairi McFarlane*

Sometimes, when my partner and I are sat side by side on the sofa of an evening, both staring at our phones, I think about how our bodies are inches away from each other but our minds are occupying different universes. That's the thing about the internet – it can bring people together, but it can also create distance.

I think of it like those giant plastic hamster balls you see at festivals. We're each inhabiting our own hamster ball and within its confines we're only ever exposed to content which is specifically designed for us – reflecting our interests, confirming our biases, connecting us with like-minded people. Knowing this is half the battle. Understanding that there is no such thing as 'the internet', really: we each have our own internet that we escape to every time we swipe to open our phones and, for the most part, algorithms decide what we will encounter there.

We've explored in this book ways to take back control from the algorithms and make conscious decisions about what your 'online wallpaper' should consist of. But we also need to acknowledge there is such a thing as objective truth. We cannot all be operating on our own set of tailored facts. For, as American writer Harlan Ellison once famously said:

'YOU ARE NOT ENTITLED TO YOUR OPINION. YOU ARE ENTITLED TO YOUR *INFORMED* OPINION. NO ONE IS ENTITLED TO BE IGNORANT'

If living life during the age of the internet has taught me one thing, it's to cherish and defer to **genuine expertise**. There's essentially two ways to become an expert: through lived experience or through extensive learning/training. It doesn't matter how many YouTube videos we watch, or blogs we read on a particular topic, we should always concede that we will never know more than people who have gained expertise through one of these two channels.

A nurse who has worked in the NHS for ten years, for example, will always be more of an expert on the NHS than you or me. A doctor who has spent years studying to gain a PhD in physics knows more about physics than you or me. We are all allowed to have an **(informed)** opinion, but it's also important we accept that our opinions are less valuable than the views held by experts on any given topic. Giving everyone's views, no matter how ill-informed, equal weight might sound like a lovely, utopian idea, but it actually leads to complete chaos, widespread disinformation, social disharmony and even death.

As we have also discovered, context is really important too. Sometimes, for example, I correct people when they introduce me as 'an expert on mental health'. I suppose, living as I do with a long-term mental health issue makes me a kind of expert by experience, but all the science that informs my talks in schools and at events and what I write in my books comes from qualified neuroscientists, psychologists and psychiatrists. If I'm an expert in anything, it's how to translate their expertise into something which is (hopefully) engaging and relevant for an audience of young people, a job I've been doing for (at the time of writing) more than thirteen years.

We've all become so afraid to say 'I don't know', fearing it will make us look ignorant, when in fact in many cases that's the smartest response. Having all the information in the world at our fingertips doesn't make us experts in everything, or indeed anything. In fact, as we have seen already, being bombarded with so much content often makes us stupider. We cling to simple narratives when we feel overwhelmed.

In order to write this book, I interviewed a range of experts to ensure I was bringing you, the reader, the benefit of views which were informed by proper experience, robust learning and objectivity. I had some fascinating conversations with people who dedicate their lives to understanding how the internet works and how it in turn impacts the way we think and behave. Each chat was enough to inspire a book in its own right and I've tried really hard to cherry-pick the most pertinent parts to form the basis of this manual. But I also wanted to bring you some wisdom direct from these experts and their quotes are peppered throughout the book (you can also find details of where to find out more about them at the back).

I hope I have been able to give you some practical tools to ensure you can enjoy the advantages of the online world, without succumbing to its many pitfalls. I hope I have asked you some questions which will make you think about the content you put out into the world and the way you receive information. Most of all, I hope I have made you realize that, whilst nothing we post to the internet can ever truly be erased, you (as someone who has likely grown up online) are allowed to evolve, change and grow. You are still finding out who you are. That involves making mistakes and trying on identities which, in retrospect, you will realize didn't really fit. That's okay. In fact, it's a crucial part of human development – something which teenagers and people in their early twenties are programmed to do.

FOR ME, ONE OF THE GREATEST DANGERS OF THE INTERNET IS THAT IT HITCHES US TO OUR PAST ERRORS IN JUDGEMENT OR BEHAVIOUR, BUT DOESN'T ALWAYS REWARD US FOR CHANGING OUR PERSPECTIVES.

Some people tend to double down because of this. They don't see the point in altering their view because they've amassed a following being the way they always were and everyone outside of their hamster ball seems to be shouting at them. Their world becomes narrower and narrower, their opinions more binary and entrenched.

That's no way to live. As Imran Ahmed from the Centre for Countering Digital Hate said, we're each in our own slipstream, coloured according to our pre-existing prejudices, but social media is a kaleidoscope. The more we can zoom out, the more we'll be able to separate the truth from the falsehoods, see behind the narratives and agendas and use the wealth of information on the web in a way that is discerning and useful.

Whilst writing this book I used social media as normal, but I also took a step back from my online interactions and thought **'What's actually going on here? And is there a pattern?'** as well as **'What advice would I give someone else if this happened to them?'**

I'd recommend having these questions in the back of your mind when you're online, too – they really changed the way I view and use apps.

USING THE TECHNIQUES IN THIS BOOK MADE ME REALIZE THAT, WHEN I CONVERSE WITH ANOTHER PERSON ONLINE, WE'RE NOT SIMPLY DISCUSSING THE TOPIC IN HAND.

IT'S THE CLASHING OF TWO TOTALLY DIFFERENT WORLD VIEWS AND BELIEF SYSTEMS, WHICH WILL LIKELY BE INCOMPATIBLE, ESPECIALLY AS THEY'RE MEETING WITHOUT ANY OF THE USUAL SOCIAL CUES WHICH WOULD ALLOW US TO CONTEXTUALIZE THE CONVERSATION.

Once it's brought to your attention, you'll notice that the knee-jerk reactions of trolls and other commentators often have absolutely nothing to do with the post they're supposedly responding to. For example, posts about racism are often met with the accusation that the person who posted them 'hates their country'. But if you unpack where that response has actually come from, it's a fear that the standards of the world are changing and that will necessitate re-evaluating past behaviour and choices. After all, as Pixie Turner said during our interview, 'everyone wants to believe they are a nice person'.

This reinforces the importance of forgiving people for their past transgressions if they genuinely seem to have learned and grown – in this way, we reward progress. It also made me think of a conversation I once had with a psychologist who said 'social media is the closest we'll ever get to observing people in a vacuum'. When we post, we are revealing much more about ourselves than we ever will about the subjects or people we are discussing.

NOW, I THINK OF MY SOCIAL MEDIA INTERACTIONS AS A FASCINATING OPPORTUNITY TO OBSERVE HUMANITY, RATHER THAN ANY KIND OF MEANINGFUL REFLECTION ON WHO I AM OR MY WORTH.

I AM HAPPIER FOR IT AND I HOPE YOU WILL BE, TOO.

TIPS AND TRICKS

AN OVERVIEW

I've sprinkled practical tips for managing your relationship with tech, the internet and social media throughout this book. I've listed most of them below, as a reminder:

AVOIDING TECH ADDICTION

- Remember you don't have to be on every app; pick the ones you find the most fun and useful and the least toxic
- Disable screen notifications
- Decide in advance how much time you want to spend playing a game or browsing an app
- Find ways to create 'space' between the urge and action of scrolling/gaming
- Set a 'digital sunset' (a time when your phone goes in a drawer/on airplane mode) about an hour before you want to go to sleep

YOUR CONTENT/OUTPUT

- If you're asking yourself the question 'should I really be posting this?' the answer is probably 'no'

- Don't post fake news unless it's very obviously a joke (so obvious, even someone who didn't know about the story/incident/people involved would realize instantly)
- Ensure everything you post is true, or at least would be deemed to be a fair opinion based on the facts, unless it is obviously a joke
- Remember: being authentic doesn't mean you are obliged to overshare. It's okay to have boundaries and only to post what you feel comfortable other people knowing

SWERVING FAKE NEWS

- Search each piece of content or question 'fresh'. Don't just watch the videos or click on the links the algorithm suggests
- If someone is speaking a lot about a 'problem' you weren't aware of before, be wary if they're also selling a 'solution'
- Check sources and whether the studies cited come from reputable publications, have a decent sample size and are peer- reviewed
- Don't assume 'traditional media' (newspapers, TV, radio) is completely impartial – whilst they have to follow more stringent guidelines, they are just as likely to have an agenda
- Use websites with a proven track record of impartiality to fact-check anything you're unsure about

WHAT TO ENGAGE WITH

- See your clicks and engagement as currency – spend it wisely, on the kind of content which nourishes you and you'd like to see more of
- Try to avoid the temptations of clickbait – it fuels the outrage economy and encourages the creation of more unethical and irresponsible content
- Don't feed the trolls. If you must share something offensive or outrageous, screenshot and anonymize where possible to avoid inadvertently amplifying their message and growing their following

WHO TO FOLLOW

- Regularly evaluate who you're following by mindfully scrolling through your feed and noticing how content is making you feel
- Seek out role models who are inspiring, positive, stimulating, entertaining and diverse
- Don't expect your online role models to be perfect – we're all human
- Follow some people outside of your 'stream' but make sure, if their opinions differ radically from your own, there is evidence for what they are saying and their motivations seem to be good
- Remember to show love and support for people whose content you appreciate

ALLYSHIP

- Don't become an ally because you think it makes you look good. Understand why it's genuinely the right thing to do (this should prevent your allyship becoming performative)
- Unless they offer, don't expect your Black/brown/gay/trans/ disabled friends to teach you how to be an ally

ACTIVISM

- Remember you can't fix all the problems in the world, or even on the internet. Pick one or two things you care about and channel your energy into those
- Have a clear call to action (what do you want supporters to do?), thoroughly research the impact of the problem you're trying to solve and, if possible, get people who can help you effect change (like lawyers and politicians) on board
- Hone your elevator pitch: people's attention spans (particularly online) are limited

DISCUSSIONS WITH PARENTS, CARERS AND TEACHERS

- Try giving your parent a virtual tour of an app or game if they don't understand it
- Ask them if you can come up with house/school rules around tech as a team
- Work out your ideal scenario in advance and then be prepared to compromise on it
- If you want them to trust you, show them that you are trustworthy

ONLINE SAFETY

- Use strong passwords
- Set up two-factor authentications on all your apps
- Don't post anything which inadvertently reveals your address or exact date of birth
- Use only secure websites where possible
- Never click on phishing links
- Always log out after each session

EMOTIONAL ONLINE SAFETY

- Mute users or hashtags if they are triggering
- Remember, you don't have to comment or come up with a take on every trending topic – it's okay to sit it out
- If you're piled on, log off for forty-eight hours, then apologize sincerely (if you are actually sorry) or don't engage
- If you are being cyberstalked, harassed or feel unsafe for any reason, report to the police

REFERENCES

INTRODUCTION

(1)   telegraph.co.uk/women/life/what-its-like-being-forced-to-read-hundreds-of-vile-online-comme

CHAPTER 1

(2)   psycnet.apa.org/record/2011-29870-001
(3)   mirror.co.uk/news/technology-science/technology/revealed-heres-how-many-times-6727470
(4)   brainyquote.com/quotes/viktor_e_frankl_160380
(5)   ico.org.uk/media/1545/cookies_guidance.pdf
(6)   bbc.com/future/article/20170926-is-porn-harmful-the-evidence-the-myths-and-the-unknowns

CHAPTER 2

(7)   bylinetimes.com/2021/03/24/home-office-fails-to-explain-strange-expenses
(8)   twitter.com/mrjamesob
(9)   twitter.com/mariannaspring
(10) counterhate.com/anti-vaxx-industry
(11) bbc.co.uk/bitesize/articles/zckbsk7
(12) theguardian.com/politics/2019/nov/20/twitter-accuses-tories-of-misleading-public-in-factcheck-row
(13) sarahmillican.co.uk/standard-issue

CHAPTER 4

(14) en.wikipedia.org/wiki/Negativity_bias
(15) en.wikipedia.org/wiki/Blackout_Tuesday

CHAPTER 5

(16) change.org
(17) bbc.co.uk/sport/football/55338104
(18) independent.co.uk/news/uk/home-news/period-poverty-campaign-free-sanitary-schools-amika-george-a9285346.html
(19) natashadevon.com/the-mental-health-media-charter
(20) wheresyourheadat.org
(21) change.org/p/amber-rudd-make-it-compulsory-to-have-a-mental-health-first-aider-at-work-wheresyourheadat
(22) heatworld.com/life/mental-health/wheres-your-head-at-parliament-2/
(23) https://www.globalplayer.com/podcasts/episodes/7DrbZrb/
(24) centreformentalhealth.org.uk/news/mental-health-problems-work-cost-uk-economy-ps349bn-last-year-says-centre-mental-health
(25) twitter.com/MHMediaCharter/status/1391707247278018565?s=20

ORGANIZATIONS

www.counterhate.com
The Centre for Countering Digital Hate is an international not-for-profit NGO that seeks to disrupt the architecture of online hate and misinformation. The Centre has offices in London and Washington DC.

www.childnet.com
Childnet International is a non-profit organization working with others to help make the internet a great and safe place for children.

www.glitchcharity.co.uk
Glitch is an award-winning UK charity that is working to end online abuse – particularly against women and marginalized people.

www.fullfact.org
Fullfact are a team of independent fact-checkers and campaigners who find, expose and counter the harm it does.

stopfundinghate.info
Stop Funding Hate make hate unprofitable by persuading advertisers to pull their support from publications that spread hate and division.

EXPERTS

Imran Ahmed is the founder and CEO of the Center for Countering Digital Hate US/UK (See 'organizations on page 201). He is an authority on social and psychological malignancies on social media, such as identity-based hate, extremism, disinformation, and conspiracy theories. He regularly appears in the press and documentaries as an expert on how bad actors use digital spaces to harm others and benefit themselves and how and why wrong platforms allow them to do so.

He advises politicians around the world on policy and legislation. Imran was inspired to start the Center after seeing the rise of antisemitism on the left in the United Kingdom and the murder of his colleague, Jo Cox MP, by a white supremacist, who had been radicalized in part online during the EU Referendum in 2016. He holds an MA in Social and Political Sciences from the University of Cambridge. Imran lives in Washington, DC.

Seyi Akiwowo is a multi award-winning founder and CEO of Glitch (See 'organizations on page 201), a former TED and international speaker, respected consultant and writer within the political and tech space. Seyi is known for her work on preventing online abuse and championing digital citizenship. In 2022, Seyi published her debut book How To Stay Safe Online, a digital self-care toolkit for developing resilience and allyship.

Dr Aaron Balick is a psychotherapist, media consultant, and author of The Psychodynamics of Social Networking. He has also published two self-help books: Keep Your Cool, for children, and The Little Book of Calm. Aaron is an honorary senior lecturer at the Department for Psychosocial and Psychoanalytic Studies at the University of Essex. Find out more: aaronbalick.com

Daniel Barnett is a barrister practising from Chambers in London, and presents The Legal Hour on LBC Radio. He has written nineteen legal textbooks and represents employees and employers in high-value, high-profile employment litigation. Find him on Youtube: https://www.youtube.com/@DanielBarnettLaw

Marianna Spring is a specialist disinformation and social media reporter for BBC News where she investigates the impact of online disinformation and conspiracy theories and the impacts they have. She was previously a BBC reporter covering breaking news geared at a younger audience and makes frequent appearances on BBC TV segments including presenting on BBC Panorama about her investigation into anti-vaccine content. Find out more: en.wikipedia.org/wiki/Marianna_Spring

Pixie Turner is a registered nutritionist (RNutr), BACP-accredited psychotherapist and science communicator. She is the brains behind the 'Pixie Nutrition' social media accounts, which aim to encourage a healthy relationship with food and debunk nutrition misinformation online. In addition, she has been featured as a nutrition expert on the BBC and Channel 5, and in publications such as *Red*, the *Evening Standard*, *Grazia*, *The Telegraph* and more.

Dr Linda Papadopoulos is a chartered psychologist and an associate fellow of the British Psychological Society. As well as an accomplished academic career where she set up and headed successful post-graduate and doctoral programmes in Psychology, she is also an active researcher and her work has informed government policy. Her comments regarding the psychology behind news and current events are often syndicated by the press and discussed by TV and radio networks both in the UK and the US. She is a regular commentator on psychological issues in broadcast, radio and print media. Find out more: drlinda.co.uk/

James Perkins worked at Full Fact, the UK's independent fact checking charity, analyzing and countering online misinformation. He now leads the social media team at LBC.

THE DEFINITIVE GUIDE TO CARING FOR YOUR MIND AND SUCCEEDING AT SCHOOL.

In this brilliant funny book, mental health campaigner Natasha Devon shows that by identifying your learning style, building resilience and remembering to take some time out and have fun you can ace school without losing your mind.

* Learn how your brain works then
sort and tackle your anxieties

* Take quizzes to find out what motivates you
to learn and tailor-make your own schedule

* Plan your free time with tips on baking,
doodling, dancing and relaxation techniques